IN THEIR CONCERN with the perennial controversy between the two great areas in which men seek knowledge, three eminent literary scholars and a distinguished jou^{...} nalist in these essays address themselves ·he que^{...}tion D^{...} ¹ ᵃ ᵇ ·r ·ᵒᵗi·

concern for his world most clearly in the myths by which man realizes his involvement in mankind and his responsibility for his own destiny.

FRANK KERMODE, professor of English, University of Bristol, argues that to follow the ways of the sciences in searching out repetitions such as make myths is to lose sight of the unique, particular, and concrete expressions which underlie personal participation and sharpen the sensibilities. And this experience, he maintains, is the peculiar contribution of the humanities.

BARRY BINGHAM, editor and publisher of the Louisville *Courier-Journal,* calls for a vigorous application of the humanities to American life. The humanities, he holds, "must show the courage to help lead out of bondage an American generation that sold its inheritance for an illusion of freedom, but has found itself enslaved by its own fears and frustration."

These essays are based upon lectures given during the Conference on the Humanities held at the University of Kentucky in October, 1965, as a part of the celebration of the University's Centennial.

THOMAS B. STROUP, the editor of this volume, is professor of English at the University of Kentucky.

THE HUMANITIES AND THE UNDERSTANDING OF REALITY

A CENTENNIAL PUBLICATION

THE HUMANITIES

AND THE

UNDERSTANDING OF REALITY

BY MONROE C. BEARDSLEY, NORTHROP FRYE,

FRANK KERMODE, AND BARRY BINGHAM

EDITED BY THOMAS B. STROUP

1966 · LEXINGTON, KENTUCKY

UNIVERSITY OF KENTUCKY PRESS

INTRODUCTION

THE FOUR PAPERS which constitute this volume were delivered as lectures at the Conference on the Humanities held as a part of the Centennial Program at the University of Kentucky on October 22-23, 1965. Some of them have been slightly revised since their delivery. The conference was one among several set up by the Centennial Committee to consider scholarly and scientific subjects or to discuss the place of each of the several broad divisions of learning in the academic order of life. The special purpose of this Conference on the Humanities was to examine afresh the qualities peculiar to the studies generally called the humanities in the belief that such reexamination would serve to stimulate a proper interest in them and their values. The title of the conference was "The Humanities and the Quest for Truth."

Its chairman in charge of arrangements was Dr. W. S. Ward, Professor of English. The lecturers were Professor Monroe C. Beardsley, Chairman of the Department of Philosophy at Swarthmore College, Professor Northrop Frye, Principal of Victoria College, University of Toronto, Professor Frank Kermode, Professor of English, University of Bristol (England), and Mr. Barry Bingham, Editor and Publisher of the Louisville *Courier-Journal*. Three general sessions and a dinner were held. At each of the general sessions one of the academic participants presented a lecture and the others commented upon it. Mr. Bingham gave the dinner speech.

The question proposed for the conference to consider and, hopefully, to answer was what distinctive contribution do the humanities make to an understanding of reality? Or, as Professor Frye put it a little less formidably, "What do the humanities provide for human culture that the sciences do not provide?" However expressed, the question is still one to intimidate all but the dauntless. Yet the speakers on this occasion, without special display of boldness but assuming a humanistic modesty in their courage, addressed themselves in their various ways to the subject. And as one must expect from humanists, their ways were different, however alike some of their conclusions.

Beginning with the observation that the question as formulated suggested a need for a defense, Professor Beardsley warned that the humanities are not now so much imperiled by their traditional opposition from the scientists as by the uncritical support of friends from all learnings and occupations. He pointed out that the social or human sciences now dispute the humanities' claim to provide the fundamental understanding of human nature; and the defense of the humanists, too often a belittling of their opponents, leads Professor Beardsley to his attempt to isolate that contribution to man's understanding which these studies alone offer. He believes that the humanities offer no special knowledge of any range of phenomena, no special normative knowledge as separate from empirical, nor any intuitive knowledge as belonging *only* to the branches of learning called *humanities*. By his process of logical elimination he drops philosophy and history as having no unique humanistic contribution, invaluable as they are to all learnings, and centers upon literature and the arts. Among these he finds that prose fiction most readily illustrates the unique contribution. It can enormously increase the ordinary person's ability to acquire knowledge about himself and be so changed in the process that he may come to a genuine understanding of himself and of other men. It leads to an awareness, a sensitivity—as do art and music and other literary forms—not otherwise come by.

Professor Frye, in contrast to Professor Beardsley, maintains that the question posed was actually a subject for study, not a problem having any solution. He points out that since Hegel philosophers have unsuccessfully tried to set up the basic difference between *Natur* and *Geist*. Reversing the question as posed, and asking what is the unique contribution of the sciences, he states with assurance that the physical sciences provide nature and that the peculiar function of these sciences is to objectify reality. They are empirical and predictable; and the social sciences, as statistically grounded, are predictable but less empirical. Philosophy and history, more purely verbal than the social sciences, nonexperimental, and nonpredictive, nevertheless depend upon the scientific amenities of accuracy, objectivity, and the dispassionate handling of evidence. And so does literary and artistic criticism. On the other hand, the arts themselves do not require these scientific methods. The assumption that if the sciences are objective, the arts must be subjective is unwarranted: the arts are techniques of communication, depending upon conventions (accepted repetitions), as do the sciences. Yet the arts are distinct: their role is "to express humanity's awareness of being itself rather than its perception of what is not itself and outside itself." Expression, not explanation, and humanity's awareness are not unlike Professor Beardsley's individual's awareness. But Professor Frye goes further. He would probe this awareness so as to discover the great unifying forces lying within the selfhood of the race. For him the study of the humanities leads to the discovery of the "containing forms, or myths" repeated in literature and the other arts from primitive times. By these a man comes to realize his involvement in mankind and his responsibility for the world he creates and lives in.

Professor Kermode directly opposes Professor Frye—in method at least. Without concern for the discovery of the underlying generic conceptions, myths and archetypes, he would develop a proper sensitivity to the "high vernacular" as necessary to the continuation of a "literary public." (The maintenance of such a public is necessary to the continuation of a humane culture.) The development of this sensitivity calls for the understanding of the paradigms of the arts, the "radical patterns of fictions," the language of the high vernacular. This "language" accomplished, the reader turns directly to a particular poem or novel or other form ready to participate in it, to re-create the particular piece in terms of the present. He has made the work relevant to himself and his generation. Thus Dante or Wordsworth or Beethoven or Michelangelo survive to nurture the present and the future generations —not by our finding out the underlying myths in their works. Not the mythic outcroppings of Freud's iceberg of the racial unconscious seem primary to Professor Kermode, but rather the immediate and direct experience based upon a knowledge of the paradigms. He holds that the humanist's critical task must be to convince the student that "if he learns the language and submits himself to the work he will discover its conformity with his own mind and the kinds of question he wants to ask." He maintains that too much attention to myths and archetypes frustrates "the act of personal participation which is the distinctive act of a literary public." To study similarities, to follow the ways of science in searching out repetitions such as make myths, is to lose sight of the unique, the particular, and the concrete expressions which furnish the experience and sharpen the sensibilities. And this experience is the unique contribution of the humanities.

Even though the speakers approached the question from different points of view and with quite different preconceptions, even though their answers were not by any means unanimous, their agreements were surprisingly frequent, especially for humanists. Even though Professor Frye and Kermode disagree about myth and archetype, they agree upon the supreme value of the studies which express "the nature of human involvement with the human world, which is essential to any serious man's attitude to life," which enables men to achieve self-awareness and sharpens their sensibilities, and which also enables them to maintain a continuum within the flux of time. Whatever the special knowledge afforded by the humanities, whatever the special methods of finding it, it is necessary to the understanding of oneself and mankind. The study of the humanities, especially art, music, and literature, does provide a unique understanding of reality. It requires an exploration of subjective reality subjectively, as Professor Frye indicates, not merely clinically. *Nosce teipsum* is apropos, not only by way of the "huge containing conceptions" emerging out of the history of the species, but also through the direct experience of literature and the arts. The affirmation of the distinctive contribution made by these studies runs from Professor Beardsley's attempt to regard literature (as representative of the humanities) from the cognitive point of view to Professor Frye's attempt to distinguish between the kinds of studies which objectify reality and the kinds which require personal engagement to Professor Kermode's insistence upon direct involvement and participation in the work as giving a unique knowledge to Mr. Bingham's eloquent call for these studies as giving a knowledge for the professions not otherwise to be had.

So it was upon the basis of the rather logical movement from Professor Beardsley's posing of the question and his direct analysis of it to find "awareness" as unique, to Professor Frye's "concern," to Professor Kermode's "participation," to Mr. Bingham's "use" that I have determined the order of these papers. It is a tenuous order, I must admit, and one perhaps not readily perceived in their oral presentation, but it seems by all odds the most logical. Mr. Bingham was not asked in the preparation of his paper to answer the question proposed for the symposium, since his was to be an afterdinner speech. Yet it fits well into the series: if one looks at the whole, one notices that we read forward from a logical analysis of the text, the question, to the application, the rhetorical *applicatio,* of the conclusion.

So far I have tried merely to suggest the leading issues developed in the papers. To deal with them more particularly would require a critique, and a critique is not the province of an introduction. But perhaps one observation is not inappropriate. Professor Beardsley suggests that the question proposed seemed to call for an *apologia,* and one may wonder why all such symposia seem to require a defense of the humanities. Professor Frye suggests that the question be reversed, and one might have applauded him had he not immediately and with unscientific assurance answered the question in one word. But one will seldom find a scientist who would even ask the question whether he *qua* scientist has a distinctive contribution to make toward an understanding of reality. Such would seem altogether heretical. And yet one may very well do so. Indeed it would be most scientific to do so. Has he anything basic that the humanist did not first speculate upon? Does he not really depend upon the logic, the concept of the judgment withheld, and the questioning of evidence developed first by the humanists? Does he pursue his studies effectively without the imagination made sharp through such vicarious experience as the arts require? It may be well for the humanists to humble themselves, for that is the greatest of virtues; they should remember, at the same time, that without their special knowledge, even without this special virtue of humility, the sciences themselves would wither and die.

Perhaps one further observation should be made. The conference, the papers, and the discussions which followed them, were extremely lively. The questions and spirited observations following each paper were not confined to the Guignol Theatre, where they were held, but have survived to be heard in the corridors, offices, and class-rooms for months afterward. And they will continue to be heard. "To enlarge and sensitize," "containing forms and myth," and "the high vernacular" are likely to be discussed widely and for a long time. They have become part of the continuum belonging to the study of the humanities, especially at the University of Kentucky.

THOMAS B. STROUP

CONTENTS

THE HUMANITIES AND
HUMAN UNDERSTANDING

By MONROE C. BEARDSLEY

DOES THE QUESTION put to this symposium suggest that something is required by way of a defense of the humanities? This cannot be because they are in perilous straits; in some ways, they have not had it so good for a long time. They receive unstinted lip service, at least, from the most respectable sources; they get enough students to keep their teachers occupied; they are held in esteem by the professional schools of medicine and engineering, which insist that the undergraduates who come their way should have been exposed to humane learning. And now we are about to have a National Humanities Foundation—signalling that even the architects of the Great Society are ready to assign them a role in the whole design.

If there is a "crisis in the humanities," as a recent book has argued,[1] it is not that they are getting a bad press. Perhaps the danger is that in this atmosphere of generous good will, they will be supported uncritically—that we will be content to fall back on old, vague, and confused slogans, that in demanding of them what they are not equipped to give, we will fail to value them for their real qualities.

I do not mean to overlook the existence of a serious conflict. It was occasioned by the rise of the human sciences (by which I mean the social sciences and psychology) to a truly scientific and professional level during the first part of this century. For these rivals have arrived on the scene to dispute the humanities' traditional claim

to provide the most significant and fundamental understanding of human nature.

This challenge has long been in the making; what is
new about it is that now we are on the verge of being able
—with the help of work done by philosophers, social
science methodologists, and critical theorists—to cope with
it successfully. But that will not be easy. For the
bitterness of the conflict is even greater than that of its
nineteenth-century predecessor and parallel. Then the
natural sciences were fighting for their rightful place
among the acknowledged and respected academic disciplines, and many of the best minds—Mill, Huxley, Arnold
—reflected on the possibility of conceiving liberal education broadly enough to embrace the scientific study of
nature, physical and biological. When Oxford conferred
honorary degrees on Faraday and Dalton, in 1832, the
Professor of Poetry and churchman, John Keble, com-
plained that the University had "truckled sadly to the
spirit of the age"—as though an interest in the laws of
chemical combination and electromagnetism were but a
passing utilitarian fad. Compare the words of another
poet, W. H. Auden, delivering his Harvard Phi Beta
Kappa Poem in 1946:

> Thou shalt not answer questionnaires
> Or quizzes upon World-Affairs,
>   Nor with compliance
> Take any test. Thou shalt not sit
> With statisticians, nor commit
>   A social science.[2]

But those who have essayed to elevate the humanities
by belittling the human sciences have not gone unchal-
lenged. One of the most vigorous replies is still Max
Eastman's lively chapter on "The Swan-song of Humane
Letters," in *The Literary Mind,* where he said that current

2

defenders of the humanities, especially literary criticism, were

fighting for the right of literary men to talk loosely and yet be taken seriously in a scientific age. . . . They are brandishing every weapon of idea they can lay hold on—brandishing God himself if they can still hang on to Him—in a vain effort to defend the prestige of humane letters against the inexorable advance of a more disciplined study of man.[3]

The greater discipline he referred to was the systematic application of scientific method to the understanding of human nature. Of course Eastman did not escape stern reproof from F. R. Leavis, whose attack (in the very first issue of *Scrutiny*) began: "Mr. Eastman . . . presents an interesting case. It is of himself that I am thinking."[4]

The nineteenth-century conflict between the humanities and the natural sciences was primarily a competition for prestige and support, and the allegiance of good minds. The present conflict, between the humanities and the *human* sciences, is a struggle for an indivisible honor—the right to be considered the proper study of man—and it has all the rancor of civil strife. Moreover, just as class consciousness played an important role in the nineteenth-century controversy, so the current one has been much exacerbated by right-wing politicians and theorists who fear in the systematic pursuit of social science (or at least in social scientists themselves) a tendency toward liberal and social-welfare politics.

It is, by the way, a pity that C. P. Snow's much-publicized attempt to revive the older controversy by dividing the field of learning into his two antagonistic "cultures" simply ignored the existence of the human sciences. At one point in his little book he says that some of his friends, historians and sociologists, told him that he had left something out of his intellectual scene, but Snow explains that any attempt to include them would subject his main thesis to excessive subtlety![5]

When we ask a question about something, X, we do not always have to provide ourselves with a definition of the term "X" in order to be sure we understand what we are talking about. But any reasonable suspicion that the term is obscure imposes an obligation upon us to try to clarify it. And no one can deny that there are obscurities in the intension of the term "humanities." It would be extremely helpful to us, in undertaking this inquiry, if this term had ever been adequately defined.

Now, we are not completely helpless if we can agree on the *extension* of the term. There are three areas of study that many people undoubtedly want to include among the humanities: philosophy, history, and the study of the arts (most especially, the study of literature). Northrop Frye has said "that literature is the central division of the humanities, flanked on one side by history and on the other by philosophy."[6]

Given a clear-cut extension for a term, it is often no great task to extract a common set of characteristics that will serve as necessary conditions for applying that term, and it may be only a little harder to select enough necessary conditions to serve as a set of sufficient conditions as well—that is, as a set that will mark off that class from all other classes. But the task of defining "humanities" has not proved so simple.

In the first place, these subjects are extremely broad and various, as a group; and one of them, philosophy, comprises a distressing variety of interests—more than any one philosopher is likely to subscribe to. Combining philosophy, history, and the study of the arts may be a convenient way of bunching departments in a small college, for administrative purposes, but that doesn't insure a fundamental rationale.

4

In the second place, when we ask what the humanities are to be contrasted with, it is much easier to say what the others have that the humanities don't have than it is to say what the humanities *do* have that is missing from the rest. For the others are all sciences—including the social sciences. What unites the workers in all the fields of social inquiry is the effort to explain some aspect or segment of human behavior—both mental and physical— through the application of scientific method (or methods) in the broad sense: that is, the procedures of generalizing from properly selected data and constructing explanatory hypotheses to be tested by the data. I don't want to imply that the social psychologist and the sociologist use exactly the same methods to answer exactly the same questions, but their basic canons of inquiry, their basic methodological commitments, and their basic ideals of consummated research, are convergent.

Thus, one *could* allow the humanities to consist of all those reasonably systematic and intensive areas of study that are not sciences. This would be a rather unsatisfactory definition, to say the least. But perhaps we are trying to go too fast. Let us ask our question in this form: what contribution to our understanding of reality is made by the three studies that, by common consent, belong in the extension of the term? But before we try to answer this question, it will be wise to pause once more—this time to consider with a little care the meaning and scope of the question itself. What kind of answer are we after in asking it?

The question before us seems to be an epistemological one—that is, a philosophical question about the legitimacy of certain claims to knowledge. Now you may wish to dispute this interpretation of the question, at once, and to say that a "contribution to understanding" is not necessarily a "claim to knowledge." I don't think this is

5

true, if it means that understanding is something utterly distinct from knowledge. No doubt, as we sometimes say, it is possible to know things without understanding them. I know, say, that the television set won't work, but I don't understand its not working. Here I know one proposition ("the set won't work") but there is some *other* proposition I do *not* know (say, "the picture tube has finally given up"). It is my lack of knowledge of the second proposition that constitutes my failure to understand the situation described by the first one. So, I would say, though there can be knowledge without understanding, there can be no understanding that is not knowledge. When you understand why the set won't work, you know what is preventing it from working.

Now, you might say, television sets are one thing, but people are different. Understanding the behavior—or misbehavior—of the former may be the same as knowing its cause; but understanding why someone steals, or dreams, or is embarrassed at a tea party, is something else. And I agree—in part. When we can explain the stealing or the dream or the embarrassment—that is, say what caused it— we have new knowledge. That's clear. And without this knowledge, we could hardly be said to understand. Yet understanding, even if it includes knowing, may be more than knowing: it may involve entering into the other's mind, sharing his feelings to some degree, putting yourself in his place so that you have the sense of being on the "inside," psychologically speaking—in a way that is rather difficult to do in the case of the television set (though the metaphorical idiom I used above, designedly, when I said "the picture tube has finally given up," embodies a little sympathy and empathy, as well as electronics). This participation in the other's mental states is sometimes called *"verstehen."*

The concept of "understanding" is a very deep and rich

one, and of course these remarks are far from exhausting its meaning. But at the moment I am chiefly concerned to make two points. The first is that in so far as the humanities can claim to give us understanding of some aspect of reality, they must also claim to give us knowledge. So I believe I was right in thinking that the question before us can be construed as an epistemological one. The second is that *"giving* us understanding" (and hence knowledge) need not be exactly the same as *"contributing* to our understanding"—just as giving someone money is not the same as contributing to his ability to earn money. I concede this distinction gladly, for I think it is in fact the key to our problem. But that will appear later.

Let us, then, take our question as a question about what special kind of knowledge is to be gained from the humanities. But what is a *kind* of knowledge?

One answer might be that a kind of knowledge is simply knowledge of a kind of thing. There are carrots and there are radishes; so there is carrot-knowledge and radish-knowledge. These useful disciplines may be somewhat circumscribed—they don't require a place in the curriculum—yet they are at least quite clearly distinguishable.

Can we characterize the humanities epistemologically as embodying knowledge of a certain range of phenomena? In some broad sense, it is often said, the humanities are concerned with man, with his acts and works, his thoughts and feelings, and their artifacts. But this is not an exclusive interest, for the same can be said for psychology and cultural anthropology, and for economics and archaeology, which are presumably not humanities, but sciences. Nor is it a universal interest among the humanities, for some of the important parts of philosophy are not concerned with human beings at all. What about those parts of metaphysics that are directed toward reality in general? What about inquiries into meaning and truth? Some

7

people might be persuaded that these branches of philosophy should be excluded from the humanities. But I know quite a few philosophers who would resist this partition of their territory.

If the humanities are not a particular kind of knowledge in the sense of being knowledge of a particular kind of thing, we might try moving to a second and deeper level. We could say that a kind of knowledge is knowledge of certain selected *properties* of things (where properties include qualities and relations). Just as the physicist, the chemist, and the physiologist all are concerned with human organisms, among other objects, and yet are concerned with different aspects of these organisms—with physical, chemical, and organic properties—so we might try to find some very broad property, or set of properties, that are the exclusive domain of the humanities. I can think of only one likely candidate for the job of effecting this division, and that is the distinction between normative and nonnormative truths—or, as it is often (though less exactly) put, the distinction between value and fact.

I think I can assume, for our present purpose, that there *are* both normative and nonnormative truths. I wouldn't want to have to try to give an adequate philosophical defense of what is called "cognitivism" in ethics and aesthetics. According to my view, it is perfectly correct to say that we know, for example, that one poem is a *better* poem than another, that one way of distributing goods or ills is more *fair* or *just* than another way, that we have an *obligation* to act one way rather than another. These are normative propositions. And I assume that they can be supported by reasons, and even good reasons, so that we can, at least sometimes, legitimately claim to know them.

Thus it might be said that what the humanities give— not *only* what they give us, and not what only *they* give us, but what they specialize in, so to speak—is normative

8

knowledge. The *subject* of the humanities would not be special, but the *aspect* of the subject would be special—we would be concerned, for example, not with what a man *does,* but with what he *ought* to do.

It is certainly reasonable to grant the importance of this distinction, and, up to a point, it is reasonable to allocate the two inquiries to different disciplines. For the considerations that bear upon the question how, let us say, medical care actually *is* distributed among our citizens are different from the considerations that bear upon the question how it is *best* distributed—even if the answers should turn out to be the same. I say "up to a point," because I do not believe that the two types of inquiry, normative and nonnormative, are completely separable, though they are distinguishable. We can answer questions about what *is* the case without determining what *ought* to be the case; but I don't see how we could possibly decide the best, or right, system of medical care without taking into account a great many pieces of nonnormative information. And this is one reason why I do not think it is at all feasible to say: "Let the sciences, natural and social, take care of the facts about the nature of things; and let us turn over to the humanities the task of discovering what is good and right—what sort of life men ought to live, what ideals of being and doing they should frame for themselves, what rules and principles most properly guide their interactions with one another." I shudder to think what sorts of answers to these basic questions would be given if all factual knowledge were set aside.

When we consider, again, the diversity of the subjects we call the "humanities," it seems even less plausible to say that providing normative knowledge is common to them than to say that it is peculiar to them. If historians sometimes make judgments about what ought to have happened, or what ought to be done, this activity is hardly a major portion of their work—and it is viewed with skepticisms by many historians. As for the study of the arts, clearly aesthetic judgment is a very significant part of it—though by no means the whole of it. Yet a good judge of aesthetic value may not be a good judge of any other kind. I see nothing inherent in the close study of poems, plays, and novels (to say nothing of landscapes and sonatas) that qualifies a man to say what is good, or right, or worthy of being sought as an end in life. If the humanist is alleged to be expert in normative judgment in general, I would certainly like to see him produce the warrant of his authority.

So the humanities, taken as a whole, do not seem to be a kind of knowledge in the second sense. But there is a third, and still deeper, answer to the question: What is a kind of knowledge? And this is the most philosophical answer of all.

Take the mystic for example, as one who claims a special kind of knowledge. He does not necessarily claim to possess the only knowledge of God (though he may); for some truths about God might be known by logical inference from observed facts. Nor does he necessarily claim to possess the only knowledge of certain *properties* of God; for it may be that the very properties he claims to know—say, the unity of God—can be established by other methods. But what he does lay exclusive claim to is precisely an epistemological *method,* a way of knowing—which means a special source of data and a special manner of extracting knowledge from that source. He claims, in short, immediate, direct intuitive insight into the nature of a supreme supernatural being. He is a religious intuitionist.

On this basic level, a particular kind of knowledge is knowledge acquired by a particular epistemological method. If we consider scientific method, in the broad sense, as an epistemological method, then all of the sciences,

10

natural and social alike, are one kind of knowledge: that is, empirical knowledge. And any claim to knowledge that is not obtained empirically—that is, by making observations, generalizing from them, constructing and testing explanatory hypotheses—will be a claim to a radically different kind of knowledge. Empirical knowledge would be one kind, and intuitive knowledge, whatever its object, would be another kind.

The most ambitious epistemological claim that can be made for the humanities is that they contribute to our understanding by sharing with us the fruits of someone's intuitive grasp of some aspect of reality (whether of man or nature)—something that we cannot ask from the empirical sciences, but would be lost without.

The question is whether this claim to a distinctive way of knowing is valid. Let us call it the *radical epistemological question.*

When we examine in all philosophical seriousness the foundations and ambitions of the three acknowledged humanities, we are driven to the conclusion that the radical epistemological question must have a very different answer for each. They are far too diverse for a single answer to serve for all.

Take philosophy. I think of it as concerned to bring into the open, by Socratic questioning, our most fundamental beliefs about ourselves and our world, in order to examine their credentials, and to insure as far as may be that they are rationally justified. In carrying out this project, philosophers can be credited with intellectual achievements of the first importance. I am tempted to say more, but it is evident that if we once opened the question: "What distinctive contribution does *philosophy* make to our understanding of reality?" we would be in for a long week-end. We would be lucky to get away with a dialogue shorter than Plato's *Republic.* If I could try

11

out an answer on you, it would be, in part, that the knowledge we get from philosophy is more of the "knowing how" sort (as when we know how to do a job or to play a game skillfully) than of the "knowing that" sort (as when we know a particular historical or mathematical fact). My reason for saying no more at the moment is this: to get to the heart of the question before us, we must set philosophy aside, and split it off from the humanities, for as I have roughly described it, it is no more affiliated with the humanities than it is with the social or natural sciences. The problems that philosophers are concerned about arise just as pressingly and pervasively out of the assumptions and results of scientific inquiry, whether into man or nature, as out of the work of historians and literary critics. And many of the problems of philosophy can arise for the ordinary man, untutored in any academic subject, who reflects upon his ordinary experience. Philosophy is *sui generis,* and belongs to no group of studies. One clue to its independent status but universal relevance is that the phrase "philosophy of—" can be placed before practically any general noun of broad application, and will make sense. There is philosophy of music, philosophy of history, philosophy of politics and of law, philosophy of physics and of biology. And there is philosophy of civil rights, of journalism, probably even of golf.

Something close to this can be said about the phrase "history of—," though fer a very different reason. Just as every set of beliefs or opinions can be examined philosophically, to get at its rational roots, if any—so every human activity has a historical dimension that can, in principle, be investigated. So there is history of philosophy and of music, of law and of biology, and *certainly* of golf.

If we were to ask, with a firm intent to obtain an answer, whether history exemplifies a special way of knowing—that question, too, could occupy us for some time. In so far as

12

the historian attempts to tell us *what* happened and *why* (or, if you prefer, *how*), he certainly promises us empirical knowledge of a perfectly familiar sort. Some philosophers of history would say that he does more: that in explaining particular historical actions he uses a kind of intuitive insight that is not used in social science; or that to discover the "meaning" of history, in some synoptic pattern like that of Spengler or Toynbee, he requires a special epistemological method. It would be interesting to discuss these issues, too, but without a historian on this panel to correct my possibly misguided statements, I am uneasy about theorizing. My own view, for what it may be worth, is that historians show no evidence of access to a trans-empirical order of knowledge. And so I wish to set this subject aside, too, and turn directly to the study of literature. Perhaps I have left this subject in an exposed position by depriving it of Professor Frye's two flankers, but I am interested to see what it can do on its own.

Now, the propositions that the student of literature establishes (and the same can be said, *mutatis mutandis*, for the student of any art) are all, broadly speaking, concerned with certain aesthetic objects. But they may be divided into two classes: (1) propositions of literary history, which are about the causes and consequences of literary works, and (2) propositions of literary criticism, which are about the internal properties of the works.

Now, in my view, in so far as the student of literature is interested in literary history, or in describing and interpreting what he finds, he relies upon plain (though by no means simple) empirical methods. His methods are not radically distinct from those used to give us any other empirical knowledge, though they may (as Robert Lane contended a few years ago) fall short in some respects of the refinements that have been achieved (he argues) by the social sciences.[7] But knowledge about literary works is empirical knowledge in the same sense as knowledge about Central African cultures, the surfaces of the planets, or the amazing physiological properties of the flatworm.[8]

So if we are looking for a unique contribution that the study of literature makes to our understanding, not simply of literature itself, but of the world outside the literary work, only one possibility remains. For criticism has a function that goes beyond its immediate concern with the literary object: and this is its ancillary function—to help us, as readers, to get out of the work itself all that it affords. Now, if the *writing* of literature is not only an act of imaginative invention, or aesthetic construction, but an act of cognition—if literary works themselves can be said to embody knowledge of a special kind—then the study of literature takes on a new epistemological significance. Though not itself a unique form of knowledge, it may serve to liberate the knowledge that is to be found in literature, and in this indirect way literary study (especially criticism) could make a contribution to our understanding.

A case can be made out for what I call the cognitive status of music and the visual arts, and (with help) I have outlined and analyzed this case elsewhere.[9] But on the face of it, an art of words seems a more likely resource, when we are in search of knowledge, that the wordless arts; and if literature does not provide such knowledge, we may feel doubtful about turning to painting and music for it. If literature *does* provide such knowledge, it is most likely to be about a certain part of reality, namely man himself. For man is what literature is always about, whatever else it may touch upon. And since of all forms of literature, prose fiction deals most explicitly and fully and centrally with human nature—with motives and actions— let us take that mode of literature as our test.

Now, it is very often remarked that novels can teach us

truths about ourselves and our kind—that, for example, E. M. Forster, in *A Passage to India,* gives us insight into the mind of the Moslem Indian, and, more generally, the psychological effects of colonialism and racial barriers. What, indeed, could be more obvious? Yet if this is a claim to a unique intuitive knowledge, the claim is surely false. This can be shown as follows.

If a psychological truth is imparted in *A Passage to India,* it cannot be merely a particular truth about the characters of that novel, who are fictional (that is, non-existent); to reach beyond the world of the work to real people, it must be a general truth. It need not be stated explicitly anywhere in the novel, though in fact Forster's novel contains a number of such generalizations, for ex: ample:

With so emotional a people . . .

[On Dr. Aziz conversing with Professor Godbole, the Hindu] the comparatively simple mind of the Mohammedan was encountering Ancient Night.

What they said and what they felt were (except in the case of affection) seldom the same.

Like most Orientals, Aziz overrated hospitality, mistaking it for intimacy.

Truth is not truth in that exacting land unless there go with it kindness and more kindness and kindness again.

Suspicion in the Oriental is a sort of malignant tumour, a mental malady, that makes him selfconscious and unfriendly suddenly; he trusts and mistrusts at the same time in a way the Westerner cannot comprehend.[10]

The truth may be present in the novel only implicitly, as something taken for granted in the motivation, but it must be grasped by the reader and extrapolated beyond the fictional world of the novel. But then this general truth

15

is subject to test by observations of real people; therefore it is empirical and provisional; therefore, whatever may be the case with the novelist himself, this truth cannot be said to be known intuitively by the reader through his act of reading. For (the characters being nonexistent) the novel gives him no evidence for the generalization.

This is the short answer to our question whether literature conveys intuitive knowledge; it is not the long (and conclusive) answer that would be provided by a philosophical refutation of the whole intuitionistic theory of knowledge.

But suppose we were to try a lesser claim—though still a significant one. Even if one has no right to claim to *know* a psychological truth simply from having derived it from a novel, perhaps the novel can give it some antecedent probability, some initial evidence. If that is so, it seems to me, then fiction must be of great importance to the psychologist, as a source and support of his discoveries. I propose to consider next, therefore, the relation between literature and psychology.

An eminent psychologist, Gordon Allport, has said that "Literature and psychology are the two primary approaches to the study of human personality, each having distinct advantages."[11] He seems to imply that they also have equal status. An eminent novelist, Thomas Mann, has made a stronger claim for literature. He scolds Freud for tediously gathering and analyzing his case-histories, when his labors could have been lightened by more attention to "previous intuitive achievements"—including the "premonitory flashes of truly Freudian insight" in Nietzsche.[12]

Freud himself often expressed admiration and envy of imaginative writers, especially novelists, for their capacity to grasp truths that the psychologist wins only by slow work.[13] For example in his analysis of Wilhelm Jensen's *Gradiva: A Pompeiian Fantasy:*

Storytellers are valuable allies, and their testimony is to be rated high, for they usually know many things between heaven and earth that are not yet dreamt of in our philosophy. In psychological insights, indeed, they are far ahead of us ordinary people, because they draw from sources that have not yet been made accessible to science.[14]

This is a strong endorsement, though the reference to "us ordinary people" is ironic, since it is not Freud that Jensen was "ahead of," but Freud's rival psychologists. Speaking again of the "creative writer," Freud adds:

The portrayal of the psychic life of human beings is actually his very special domain; he has always been the precursor of science and of scientific psychology.[15]

But even if Freud was not in a playful mood when he paid this handsome compliment, we may be skeptical. What authority, after all, does the "storyteller" have as a purveyor of *knowledge* about human beings? Why is his testimony to be given any weight at all? If we are really interested in understanding, say, the Moslem Indians under British rule, should we not shut the novel and turn to the man who is equipped to give us (or at least get us) an answer—namely, the social psychologist?

Of course, once he has made his study and shown how both the British rulers and their Indian subjects were hurt, in different ways, then the skillful novelist can borrow his conclusions and invent a fable to illustrate them. This kind of thing has certainly been done by a sizable number of our contemporary novelists, but if it is a contribution at all (and sometimes it is), it is not a contribution to the acquisition of knowledge but to its popular diffusion. The work turns out to be either fictionalized case history or psychological science fiction. It is not by such means that literary psychology can deserve to be placed on the same level as scientific psychology—much less on a higher one.

Even if the characters and events in a novel were not invented to illustrate psychological principles, they may happen to serve as examples of them. Once he has established a certain generalization about human behavior—say Freud's theory about the causation of neurosis—the psychologist may find a fictional case that turns out to be a better example than any of his real ones. Just because it is made up, it may exhibit the development of a particular neurosis in a purer form; it may have all the characteristic features—some of which are lacking in most actual cases—and fewer incidental irrelevancies. And for teaching purposes, it may be ideal: a textbook example.

Thus Freud, in his paper on "Some Character-Types Met with in Psycho-Analytic Work,"[16] makes ingenious use of Lady Macbeth and of Rebecca, in Ibsen's *Rosmersholm*, to illustrate the person who is "wrecked by success." Each woman turns away from the fruits of her ambition just as they become ripe, and Freud is interested in the question why they do this. Rebecca's guilt he traces back to the domination of the Oedipus complex, treating her, as he says, "as if she were a living person and not a creation of Ibsen's imagination."[17] And his analysis is very illuminating. But it is essential to note here what comes first and what second. Freud has already established his theory; the story is only an example. If the theory had been based solely on the study of fictional characters and their behavior, it would, of course, have no scientific value at all, for, since all the supporting cases would be nonexistent people there would (strictly speaking) be no evidence for it. It would be like a theory of evolution based solely on the medieval bestiary and early travellers' yarns about exotic animals.

But if a fictional case can serve as illustration of a theory, then it might have been capable of suggesting the theory in the first place. To pursue this important line of thought, we must look a little more deeply into the nature of psychological discovery.[18] The essential object of the psychologist's inquiry is not a mere particular description, however elaborate, nor yet a generalization about groups of people, but something else, not so easy to describe. The best term I can find for it is "psychological mechanism." Though the connotations of "mechanism" may be repellent, let us try to lay them aside. Consider the concept of repression. It is the concept of a certain way the mind might work, a form of mental functioning or dynamics, a particular pattern of activity—that is what I mean by a "psychological mechanism."

To discover a psychological mechanism is, in the first place, to think of it as a possibility and formulate it clearly; and, in the second place, to establish its existence by showing how it helps to explain some segment of actual human behavior in at least one case. The psychologist may, of course, be interested to know how widespread the mechanism is, and the value of his discovery will depend in part upon the range of human behavior it can help to explain. Much of the important work done by psychologists will consist in applying the concept—in generalizing about it. But it is not too much to say that the genius of the great psychologist, like Freud, lies especially in his capacity to discover new psychological mechanisms.

Note that I am pressing a sharp distinction here between the mechanism itself and generalizations about it. It is one thing to conceive of a person as, for example, reacting to his own embarrassment by behaving even more embarrassingly. You remember Dr. Aziz at Fletcher's well-meant tea party in *A Passage to India*—"all shoddy and odious. . . . He did not mean to be impertinent to Mr. Heaslop. . . . He did not mean to be greasily confidential to Miss

Quested, only to enlist her support; nor to be loud and jolly towards Professor Godbole."[19] Here is a psychological mechanism, which the novel makes us see very clearly in action—more clearly than we would see it if we were present. It is quite another thing to discover that this mechanism frequently occurs, or that Orientals or colonial people are more subject to it than others. A psychological mechanism can be named by a noun or by a participial phrase, "reacting to one's own embarrassment by behaving even more embarrassingly." A generalization is expressed in a declarative sentence, or clause: "Most people of such-and-such a sort exhibit this psychological mechanism," or "Most behavior of such-and-such a sort can be explained by this mechanism."

It is in this quarter, then, that it seems most promising to look for the special psychological value of fiction. It is quite possible that some highly original literary works have described psychological mechanisms that had not till then been noticed by psychologists. The curious fact is that, though it is easy to think of might-have-beens, it is apparently impossible to discover actual instances. One might-have-been is the case of Stavrogin in Dostoyevsky's novel *The Possessed* (or *The Devils*). In that nightmarish section, "At Tihons," which was deleted from the original version (1872) after it was in proof, Stavrogin makes his "confession" to the monk, and comes to realize that he has an unconscious wish for martyrdom. Being driven to "self-lacerating" behavior by an unconscious wish for martyrdom—here is an interesting psychological mechanism. If this section of the novel had been published in 1872, a pre-Freudian psychiatrist could have read it and wondered whether a similar mechanism was not at work in one of his own recalcitrant patients. If he had then employed the concept successfully in explaining this patient's behavior, we could say that Dostoyevsky's novel had contrib-

20

uted to psychology by suggesting a possible psychological mechanism whose existence was later verified.

When we search for actual, rather than hypothetical, examples of this sort of assistance, we are balked.[20] Freud, for example, took much pride in the psychological mechanism that he discovered and called the "Oedipus complex," and in the letter in which he first referred to it,[21] he discussed both Oedipus and Hamlet. But he did not claim to have gotten the idea from Sophocles or Shakespeare; it came up, in fact, during his self-analysis, on which he was engaged at the time. It is true that the following month he wrote "I can only analyze myself with objectively acquired knowledge."[22] But this "objective" knowledge apparently came from the study of his patients, not from literature.

Since *Delusion and Dream* is Freud's completest analysis of a literary work, and a most remarkably subtle and acute one, it might be expected to provide an example, if any exists, of psychological mechanisms originally suggested to Freud by literature. The quotations I gave earlier about the storyteller being a valuable ally, and a "precursor of science and of scientific psychology," make a strong claim, which Freud puts even more specifically. He assures us that Jensen's novel embodies Jensen's knowledge of the mechanism of repression, and its connection with delusions—a mechanism which, as Freud demonstrates so brilliantly, the novel perfectly illustrates. Freud's contemporary psychologists, he says,

have still to learn what Jensen knows very well—that there are psychic processes which, despite the fact that they are intensive and show vigorous activity remain far removed from consciousness.[23]

Jensen has grasped and represented the ever-present chief characteristic of the morbid psychic processes.[24]

21

And Freud poses the question: "How had the author acquired the same knowledge as the physician, or, at any rate, what enabled him to behave as if he possessed it?"[25]

It is by no means easy to make clear and consistent sense of what Freud says. At one point he argues that since the application of his own

rules of dream-interpretation to Hanold's first dream has succeeded in making this dream comprehensible to us in its chief features and in fitting it into the sequence of the story . . . it must have been produced by its author with due consideration for these rules.[26]

But later he says

We think that our author needed to know nothing of such rules and intentions, so that he may disavow them in good faith. . . . Our author proceeds in another way [than Freud himself]; he directs his attention to the unconscious in his own psyche, is alive to its possibilities of development and grants them artistic expression. . . . But he does not need to express these laws, need not even recognize them clearly; they are, as a result of the tolerance of his intellect, contained incarnate in his productions.[27]

The "laws" and "rules" that Freud refers to are to be understood, I think, precisely as what I have been calling psychological mechanisms. Freud does not seem to be quite sure just how to describe Jensen's cognitive relation to these mechanisms. He wants to say that Jensen "knows very well"—has "grasped"—something that other psychologists don't know, but surely this is putting it too strongly. We cannot infer that Jensen knows anything about repression in real people, just because he can make up a fictitious character who exhibits it. He has *invented* a psychological mechanism, but he hasn't *discovered* it, in the full sense, because he has not yet employed that concept in explaining the behavior of any actual person. That task is left for Freud himself. And Freud is quite clear in other places that a proposed mechanism must be put to empirical test, and is not knowledge in the full sense until it has been.[28]

One can understand Freud's pleasure in being able to taunt his skeptical colleagues: Look, you couldn't find the truth, as I have, though even an untrained novelist has found it. And that accounts for his suggestion that if they couldn't discover the mechanism of repression by studying their patients, they might have discovered it (or at least made its acquaintance) by reading the *Pompeiian Fantasy*.[29] But that, of course, is going too far. For the concept was not really formulated by the novelist; its actual working was not analyzed and defined. All that Jensen really did is present the story of a young man whose remarkable behavior can be beautifully explained in terms of this concept. But if the mechanism of repression is embodied in the fictitious character in the same way as it would be in an actual neurotic, then the same analytic procedure (and psychological genius) will be required to understand Hanold as Little Hans.[30] It looks, in short, as though Freud could not really have found repression in *Gradiva* unless he had already found it elsewhere.

But that is not the whole story. The refinement and elaboration of a complex and powerful new concept, such as that of repression, may be a long process, during which the concept may be shaped by many influences. At this stage of his inquiry, the psychologist must be alert to all sorts of possibilities, thinking of ways in which the concept can be sharpened, or broadened to various sorts of human behavior. And it may well be that Freud's wide and constant reading in literary works, eager as he was to think psychologically about the characters he encountered in them, played its role in helping him to formulate more clearly and deeply the psychological mechanisms he was evolving and testing. For his own purposes, indeed, the psychologist may use literature a little roughly, in that he is only interested in some aspects of it. But his ruthlessness will not hurt it if we know what he is up to. He may come up with some weird interpretations, from the literary critic's point of view, for some works of fiction will illustrate psychological mechanisms best when parts of them are ignored or distorted to make them fit.[31] But if the reader is misled, it is the critic's job to set him straight. If we are guided by a sound critical theory we will bear in mind that a "psychological interpretation" of a literary work (that is, the use of it to illustrate a concept in scientific psychology) is often a very different thing from interpretation in the literary critic's sense—which is simply the process of finding out what it actually means.

It may well be unreasonable to expect prose fiction to prove its cognitive worth by serving the professional interests of the psychologist. The test may be too tough. So let us turn, finally, to the ordinary person who feels—and testifies—that his understanding is enlarged by reading fiction, though the characters are nonexistent and the author no psychologist. How, we may ask, does fiction contribute to human understanding?

Here is the answer given by Simon O. Lesser:

We read primarily to discover ourself—above all, perhaps, to discover what St. Augustine refers to as the dark corners of the heart. We want to know what we would be like if circumstances offered a particular propensity more scope, the form our life might take if we were less intimidated by prudential considerations, if we were more honest and more passionate, or possibly more cunning and predacious, than we are in our everyday life. We want to know how we would actually feel and behave if we were placed in this or that situation.[32]

24

Two different views are suggested here. "What we *would* be like," "how we *would* actually feel"—these verbs surely claim too much. No novel can really give me evidence for a prediction about my own behavior. But "the form our life *might* take" refers to possibilities—that, like Lord Jim, I can picture myself as being brave and cool in desperate emergencies, or that I can picture myself as being, like Lord Jim, tempted into jumping at the critical moment. It is this second view, presumably, that Mr. Lesser is advancing.

I believe there is some truth in that view though it is not the whole, or even the main, truth. There is a sense in which many of my own feelings are unknown, or but dimly known, to me. And perhaps, as Mr. Lesser has pointed out,[33] when we read fiction we are freed from certain restraints of ordinary life, and made less self-conscious; we can examine feelings and ideas more freely and frankly, more objectively, when they first appear not as our own but as those of a fictitious character. Then, having passed through this discipline, we may be able to face ourselves, and open, at least a little, those "dark corners of the heart." But I do not know how far this self-examination really goes, or can be promoted merely by reading fiction. I do not see how this could be what we read for "primarily," for it seems plain that whatever we discover about ourselves with the help of fiction, there is much more that we discover about others.

For one thing, the variety of new and unfamiliar kinds of behavior and traits of character that may pass before us in a work of fiction, gives us a widened sense of the possibilities—the potential range of humanity. This has often been said.[34] But most important of all, literature is an exercise in understanding. Even though psychologists may in fact seldom have learned of new psychological mechanisms from reading novels, the common reader becomes acquainted for the first time with precisely such mechanisms. Literature, by giving us concrete cases of understanding (fictitious) behavior, increases enormously our repertoire of explanatory concepts, so to speak—the concepts of possible mental processes that we carry about with us in our daily encounters with one another. We acquire greater skill in explaining to ourselves why people (including ourselves) do the things they do.

To write fiction is to put together plausible descriptions of human traits and human behavior. The writer himself does not always know why some of them seem obscurely to go together—why it seems that a person of a certain sort would act in a certain way. But it is up to him to create psychologically coherent characters, however complex or volatile—or at least to convince us that the traits can go together, that the actions, however diverse or even opposed, could proceed from the same person under different pressures and temptations. He shows us what looks like a possibility: a psychologically feasible combination of traits and actions. But he also shows us possible explanations of those actions. This is the important truth tucked away in a remark of Freud's (above), where he speaks of the author of *Gradiva* not only as attending to "the unconscious in his own psyche," but more importantly (and more correctly, I believe) as being "alive to its possibilities of development."

What we bear away with us from the novel is the thought that, for example, embarrassing behavior like that of Dr. Aziz can itself be the result of embarrassment; that a man can do disgraceful things because unconsciously he craves humiliation; that a boy can become a killer because through his bringing-up he has come to hate himself. We might never have realized these possibilities before. Later, when we see someone behaving in a puzzling way that reminds us of Dr. Aziz at the tea party, we are open to a

new suggestion: "Maybe he's embarrassed." We don't
know yet that he's embarrassed; we haven't learnt from
the novel any general rule by which we can leap to this
conclusion. But we can now entertain the hypothesis.
And guided by it, we may be led to further observations
that confirm its truth. In this way, I believe, fiction helps
to dispel that blindness to what is in one another's hearts
of which William James wrote, that callousness and nar-
rowness (especially with those from a strange land or of
another race) that comes from incapacity to imagine
mental states other than those we are familiar with:
impulses more generous than our own, hurts we have
never suffered, terrors that have no parallel in our own
protected lives.

Nor, perhaps, does it matter very much if some of the
psychological mechanisms invented by novelists, or some
of the combinations of traits and actions they describe,
are not psychologically possible, and do not occur in real
life—if, say, Daisy Miller "couldn't possibly have been at
all," as a friend of Henry James told him.[35] Actually, this
particular doubt seems to have proceeded from rather
limited experience. But even if it were justified, the novel
would still do something for us. Thinking that such a
person *might* exist, we would go about, so to speak, tuned
to this frequency as well as others. Our sensitivity, our
range of imagination in dealing with other people, might
still be increased.

Such is my answer to the question that was proposed.
Or at least to the part of the question that remained after
I whittled some of it away. I have reached two conclusions: first, that literature (and most especially fiction)
does contribute to our understanding of human nature,
not by presenting propositions that are radically distinct
from scientific propositions in their nature and prove-
nance, but by enlarging our powers; and second, that

therefore, in so far as the "enabling act of criticism," as it has been called, helps literature to do its proper work better, literary study indirectly makes a contribution to our understanding of human nature.

I do not in any way want to suggest that this is *all* that literature does—or all that makes literary study worthwhile. The question was not: What good are the humanities? Or even: What good is literature? The answer to these questions would be another story—and a far longer one, of course. Even if literature contributed nothing to our understanding of human nature—and I believe that some fine literary works have a negligible value from this point of view—its existence might still be thoroughly justified, and its appearance in the world very welcome. As a pattern of actions interwoven and shaped into something worthy of intense contemplation for the sake of its expressiveness and beauty, a literary work can hold up its head. Something can be said on its behalf by a reasonable aesthetic. But our duty was to set these other considerations aside for the time being, and to regard the literary work from one point of view alone: the cognitive point of view. And it seems to me clear, whatever else may be said or left unsaid, that the capacity of literature to perform this function for us—to broaden and refine our ability to understand one another—is at least one of its fairly central and lasting values.

REFERENCES

1 *Crisis in the Humanities,* ed., J. H. Plumb, Baltimore, Md.: Penguin Books, 1964. (The picture of present-day philosophy that is presented in this book is extremely one-sided.)

2 "Under Which Lyre: A Reactionary Tract for the Times" (1946), *Nones,* London: Faber and Faber, 1952. Cf. the violent denunciation of social science by another poet, Karl Shapiro, in "Why Out-Russia Russia?" *New Republic,* June 9, 1958 (with reply, June 23, 1958).

3 *The Literary Mind*, N. Y., London: Scribners, 1931, pp. 16, 30.

4 *Scrutiny*, I (May 1932), p. 20.

5 See *The Two Cultures and the Scientific Revolution*, N. Y.: Cambridge U. Press, 1959, pp. 9-10. And see the sharp criticism of Snow's scheme by Lloyd Fallers, "C. P. Snow and the Third Culture," *Bulletin of the Atomic Scientists*, XVII (1961): 306-10.

6 *Anatomy of Criticism*, Princeton: Princeton University Press, 1957, p. 12.

7 See Robert E. Lane, *The Liberties of Wit; Humanism, Criticism, and the Civic Mind*, New Haven and London: Yale University Press, 1961.

8 See the selections from the *Worm Runners Digest* in *The Worm Returns*, ed. J. V. McConnell, Englewood Cliffs: Prentice-Hall, 1965.

9 See *Aesthetics: Problems in the Philosophy of Criticism*, N. Y.: Harcourt, Brace and World, 1958, ch. 8; cf. *Philosophical Thinking: An Introduction* (with Elizabeth L. Beardsley), N. Y.: Harcourt, Brace and World, 1965, ch. 8.

10 *A Passage to India*, N. Y.: Harcourt, Brace, 1924, pp. 65, 76, 112, 142, 245, 279-80.

11 Gordon W. Allport, in his introduction to Jean Evans, *Three Men*, N. Y.: Knopf, 1954, p. viii.

12 "Freud and the Future," in *Essays of Three Decades*, N. Y.: Knopf, 1947, p. 412. Cf. Simon O. Lesser's discussion of the sense in which Dostoyevsky had "unconscious" psychological "knowledge," in "The Role of Unconscious Understanding in Flaubert and Dostoyevsky," *Daedalus*, Spring 1963, pp. 363-82 (esp. pp. 376-77).

13 See Ernest Jones, *The Life and Work of Sigmund Freud*, N. Y.: Basic Books, III (1957), 418-19; cf. I (1953), 346. See also his remarks about C. F. Meyer's novel, *The Monk's Wedding*, in a letter to Wilhelm Fliess, July 7, 1898 (*The Origins of Psychoanalysis* [letters to Fliess], Garden City: Doubleday Anchor, 1957, p. 261).

14 *Delusion and Dream*, ed. Philip Rieff, Boston: Beacon Press, 1956, p. 27.

15 *Ibid.*, p. 65.

16 *Complete Psychological Works*, Vol. XIV, London: Hogarth, 1957.

17 *Ibid.*, p. 329.

18 Without implicating him in my argument, I would like to thank my colleague, Solomon E. Asch, for criticisms and suggestions—especially on this point—from which this paper has greatly benefited.

19 *A Passage to India*, p. 77.

20 A possible, though uncertain, example is Alexander F. Shand, *The Foundations of Character*, London: Macmillan, 1926. He not only uses three literary misers (Molière's *L'Avare*, Balzac's *Eugenie Grandet*, and Gogol's Tchitchikov in *Dead Souls*) as illustrations of one of his "laws of character" ("Every sentiment tends to form a type of character of its own"; see pp. 123-26), but says that literature provided him with a great

many of "the facts or observations of character" (viii; cf. 73, 80) that he needed in exploring the possibility of a science of character or "Ethology" as defined by Mill (see the latter's *System of Logic,* Book VI, ch. 5).

21 To Fliess, October 15, 1897, in *The Origins of Psychoanalysis,* pp. 224-28.

22 Letter to Fliess, November 14, 1897; *ibid.,* p. 237. Claire Russell and W. M. S. Russell say that Sophocles' *Oedipus Tyrannus* "deceived Freud into the belief that a human male naturally and inherently wants to marry his mother and kill his father"—this "Oedipal fantasy" being in fact (according to their view) a defense against recognition of parental hostility and exploitation (see their *Human Behavior,* Boston, Toronto: Little, Brown, 1961, p. 389; cf. 485-93). If this hard-to-believe statement is true, here is at least an example of literature suggesting a *false* hypothesis— that is, describing a mechanism that *cannot* be generalized to most people. Their discussions, by the way, of this play and of *Hamlet* (chs. 8, 9) are interesting and original examples of the use of literature to illustrate psychological theories (cf. p. 423).

23 *Delusion and Dream,* p. 69.

24 *Ibid.,* p. 75.

25 *Ibid.,* p. 77.

26 *Ibid.,* p. 85.

27 *Ibid.,* pp. 116-17.

28 See *ibid.,* p. 104, p. 111.

29 Perhaps they could even have encountered it in Plato's famous passage on wish-fulfillment in dreams—where he speaks of desires "which bestir themselves in dreams, when the gentler part of the soul slumbers and the control of reason is withdrawn; then the wild beast in us, full-fed with meat or drink, becomes rampant and shakes off sleep to go in quest of what will gratify its own instincts. As you know, it will cast away all shame and prudence at such moments and stick at nothing. In phantasy it will not shrink from intercourse with a mother or anyone else . . ." (*Republic* IX, 571; trans. Cornford).

30 See Freud's "Analysis of a Phobia in a Five-Year-Old Boy," *Complete Psychological Works,* London: Hogarth, III (1925).

31 I have in mind, of course, Edmund Wilson's "ambiguity of Henry James," the theory that explains the apparitions in *The Turn of the Screw* as delusions of the governess. An even more fantastic example may be found in a most interesting anthology edited by Caroline Shrodes, Justine Van Gundy, and Richard W. Husband, *Psychology Through Literature,* N. Y.: Oxford University Press, 1943. In their bibliography they describe Joseph Conrad's story, "The Secret Sharer," in this fashion: "A projection of the inner conflicts of a schizophrenic personality is revealed in an objective narrative. The man's feelings of guilt, his withdrawal from others, and his hallucinations are finally resolved in his assumption of responsibility" (p. 384).

32 Simon O. Lesser, *Fiction and the Unconscious*, Boston: Beacon Press, 1957, p. 253.

33 *Ibid.*, p. 81, pp. 171ff.

34 It is said eloquently, for example, by T. H. Green in his essay "An Estimate of the Value and Influence of Works of Fiction in Modern Times" (1862), *Works*, 1891, vol. III—despite his definite reservations about the novel on other scores.

35 See his preface to *Daisy Miller*, in *The Art of the Novel*, ed. R. P. Blackmur, N. Y.: Scribner's, 1934, p. 270.

SPECULATION AND CONCERN

By NORTHROP FRYE

As I UNDERSTAND it, I am being asked to discuss the question: What do the humanities provide for human culture that the sciences do not provide? My own field is literature, and literature seems to belong to two groups: the creative arts, including music and painting, and the verbal disciplines, including history and philosophy. Both may be regarded as humanities, but we have to distinguish them even when we associate them. The question itself is, I suppose, legitimate enough: it is, I take it, simply a matter of trying to indicate the different functions of different things. It is difficult, and perhaps impossible, to contrast the arts and the sciences without a good deal of oversimplifying and making some false or half-true antitheses. There may be some value in oversimplifying the contrast, if one has to do that to make it at all: a more serious difficulty is that nobody is likely to approach such a problem with his mind fully made up, his convictions firmly held, and his tentative and exploratory notions outgrown. In what follows I am thinking aloud, expecting the kind of indulgence that is accorded to such improvisation.

It will not have escaped your notice that I have so far said nothing except "harrumph." But there is something to be said for the convention of beginning with an apology, or topos of modesty. This kind of question is often called, as I have just called it, a "problem," and one expects a problem to be solved. A genuine problem is a specific formulation of experience that can be adequately stated in other terms: to use a common analogy, it is like a knot in a rope that can be untied or retied without affecting the identity of the rope. A question like this is only metaphorically a problem: it is actually a subject of study, and the word solution is not appropriate. All I can do with a subject of study is to individualize it, to make a suggestion or two about how it looks from the standpoint of a literary critic who is living in the midtwentieth century.

As a subject of study, the question can hardly be called new: a whole line of philosophers from Hegel onward have beaten their brains out over the difference between the knowledge of science and the knowledge of what the Germans call *Geist,* and over the methods and techniques appropriate to the study of history or sociology as distinct from biology or chemistry. It is an appropriate question for a centennial celebration, because it was one of the liveliest issues being debated when the University of Kentucky was founded. The level of debate has not improved notably in tone since then. No contemporary treatment of the subject known to me matches the lucidity of Walter Bagehot's *Physics and Politics,* published in 1867, or the amiable and urbane discussion of Arnold and Huxley about the proportioning of humanities and sciences in the curriculum of a liberal education. A few years ago we had the Leavis-Snow dispute, where neither contribution was in the least amiable or urbane, and where it is hard to say which of the two documents was the more stupefyingly wrongheaded. Other essays purporting to defend the humanities have all too often a querulous and self-righteous air, like that of a strip-tease performer who informs a newspaper reporter that while all the other girls just take off their clothes, she is an authentic artist. And so, after more than a century of

33

giving answers to the question of what is distinctive about the humanities, it is still quite possible that the real answer is "nothing at all." Freud concludes his *Future of an Illusion* by saying: "Science is not an illusion, but it would be an illusion to suppose that we could get anywhere else what it cannot give us." He was talking about religion, but he may be unconditionally right, beyond the limits of his context, and everything nonscientific, except possibly the creative arts, may be only prescientific or pseudo-scientific. And the arts may be an exception only because their function may be a purely ornamental or decorative one. This conference, after all, deals with "The Humanities and the Quest for Truth," and the arts not only never seem to find truth, but do not even appear to be looking for it very seriously.

The best way to approach our question, I think, is to begin by reversing it, as Freud's phrasing suggests. What does science provide for human culture that the arts and the humanities do not provide? The traditional answer, and doubtless the right one, is "nature." What I am saying here is that science gives us nature, not the understanding or conception of nature. That may only be bad grammar, but I mean something more than understanding. The human mind can operate in different ways, but one very obvious way for it to operate is as a subject. That is, it can start by saying: Here am I, and I am here. Everything else is there. As soon as the mind does this, nature springs into being, like Athene from Jove's forehead, and reality appears to the mind as objective, as a field. It seems to me that it is peculiarly the function of science to objectify reality, to present the world in its aspect of being there. The world of science is the world of space: as has often been noted, science deals with time as a dimension of space. The subject itself becomes an object in this process, for there is nothing inside the scientist, from the structure of his spine to his infantile complexes, which is not also available for scientific study. Everything is there: nothing is really here except the consciousness with which he studies nature. And this consciousness, or scientific intelligence, is ideally disembodied. The theory of physics, for example, has been complicated, in its more rarefied aspects, by the fact that the scientist possesses a body, and cannot comprehend nature without physical contact. To see the world as an objective field of operation is also to quantify reality, to make it something measured rather than simply seen or heard. Isaiah praises a God "Who hath measured the waters in the hollow of his hand, and meted out heaven with the span, and comprehended the dust of the earth in a measure, and weighed the mountains in scales, and the hills in a balance." In science man takes over this traditional function of God, replacing the divine balance by the mathematician's equations.

Because science deals with reality as objective, there is no such thing as subjective science. What this means in practice is that science stabilizes the subject. It assumes a mind in the situation that we think of as sane or normal, ready to accept evidence and follow arguments. Thus science assumes a mind to some extent emancipated from existence, in the state of freedom or detachment that we call clarity. The sense of truth as an ideal, and of the pursuit of truth for its own sake as a virtue, go with the process of objectifying reality on which science is founded. The word truth itself carries with it the sense of a recognition of what is there. So does the sense of facts as given, as irreducible data to be studied in their inherent arrangements instead of being arranged. There may actually be no facts of this kind, but it is important to pretend that there are, that facts lie around immovably where they have been thrown, like rocks carried down by a glacier. As Wallace Stevens says:

The arrangement contains the desire of
The artist. But one confides in what has no
Concealed creator.

What science stands for in human life, then, is the revolt
of consciousness against existence, the sense of his own
uniqueness in nature that man gets by drawing his mind
back from existence and contemplating it as a separated
thing. The animal is immersed in existence without
consciousness; the human being has consciousness, and
consciousness means being capable, up to a point, of seeing
existence as external to oneself. Of course to withdraw
from existence means to stop existing, and some philosophers, notably Sartre, even go so far as to associate consciousness with nothingness or nonbeing. However, it
seems clear that conscious human beings can externalize
their world and still go on living. Human existence, then,
is a complex of which consciousness is one of many functions, and the concentrated consciousness that produces
science is a stylizing or conventionalizing of human behavior.

I do not wish to suggest that science is founded on a
narrowly empirical view of the world: that its end is only
to describe and understand what it sees. The physical
sciences at least are not simply descriptive, but are based
on prediction as well: they see their phenomena in time—
or their version of time—as well as space, and their end is
rather a vision of nature under law. It is not the experiment but the repeatable experiment that is the key to the
understanding of nature in the physical sciences, and the
repeatable experiment is what makes prediction possible,
and gives to science a prophetic quality. Telepathic communication, poltergeists, mediums, have been approached
experimentally and certain typical phenomena recur, but
the experiments are not repeatable (except when they are

fraudulent), no laws can be established, and so science applied to such things never gets off the ground. Where the phenomena are unconscious or where the units involved are small and numerous, like atoms, molecules or cells, so that there is no practical difference between the highly probable and the certain, the language of science is primarily mathematical. From the natural sciences we move toward the social sciences, where the phenomena are relatively large, few, and complicated, like human beings. Here prediction on a statistical basis is as important as ever, but, except for some aspects of psychology, the repeatable experiment is no longer at the centre of the study. In proportion as this is true, the subject tends to be organized verbally rather than mathematically. We then move into what are generally regarded as the humanities. History and philosophy are almost purely verbal, non-experimental, and nonpredictive. But accuracy of statement, objectivity of description and dispassionate weighing of evidence, including the accepting of negative evidence, are still required. Hence a scientific element is still present in them that distinguishes history from legend, philosophy from rumination, and, as I think, literary criticism from a good many of the activities that go under that name. From there we move into the creative arts proper, where the requirements even of accurate descriptive statement and the basing of conclusions on fair evidence are no longer made, or at least not in the same way, and where therefore we may feel that we have finally escaped from science. But except for the arts, which pose separate problems, all scholars, whatever their fields, are bound by the same code of honour. All of them have to be as scientific as the nature of their subjects will allow them to be, or abandon all claim to be taken seriously.

The philosophers who moved from Kant and Hegel towards the establishing of modern historical and sociological methods were largely preoccupied with the question of boundary lines. At what point does *Natur* turn into *Geist*? Precisely where do the methods that work in the physical sciences cease to become effective or appropriate? But it is surely possible that there are no boundary lines at all, and that this whole way of looking at knowledge as divided into two complementary bodies is wrong. The crudest form of this view is the one that I call the heart-of-darkness theory. It is a type of argument that used to be fashionable in natural theology (perhaps still is), and has been transferred to the humanities from there. There have been theories among religious apologists that religion, like the ghost of Hamlet's father, or the dancing fairies of Milton's Nativity Ode, belongs to a dark preserve of mystery on which the sun of science has not yet risen. Religion, according to this approach, deals with whatever seems at the moment to be beyond the capacities of science: creation at first, then the origin of life or the human soul, then moral values, and so on—it has to keep moving fairly fast, like the lunatic in Blake's "Mad Song," to make sure of staying in the dark while science pursues it. Even yet there is a strong popular belief that if we once get hold of something that "science cannot explain," whether it is extrasensory perception or the principle of indeterminacy or finding underground water with a hazel twig, we have a guarantee of free will and immortality and the existence of God.

The basis of such notions, when applied to the arts, is the assumption that if science deals rationally, factually, impersonally with an external world, the arts can only deal with an inner world of emotion, personality, and value. This really reduces itself to the assumption that if science is objective, the arts must be subjective. But subjective art is as impossible a conception as subjective science. The arts are techniques of communication: they are fostered by schools and groups and depend on convention quite as much as science does. In fact there seems to be nothing that is really subjective except a rebellion against the stability of the attitude toward the world on which science is based. It is very tiring to keep on being open to involuntary sense impressions, to be detached and clear-headed, to weigh evidence and fit judgments to it, and very easy to relapse into an emotional coloring of experience, such as we get from daydreaming or bad temper or private memories and associations. But however important and normally human in itself, the individual's emotional coloring of his own experience is not what the arts or the humanities are primarily concerned with. So whenever I read critical theories that begin by saying, in effect, "Poetry is whatever mere science isn't," I flake out very quickly, because I know that some version of the subjective fallacy is about to follow.

The genuine basis of this complementary view of the arts and sciences is the distinction, already glanced at and most elaborately set out in Bergson, between time as externalized by science, where it is really a dimension of space, and time in its other form of the continuous awareness of one's own existence. This latter does elude science, so here is something that science cannot explain. But nothing else can explain it either, so that is not much help. All explanation contains some traces of scientific method, unless the explanation is really a clouding up of the question, like the doctor's explanation in Molière that opium puts people to sleep because it has a dormative faculty. But while the direct awareness of being cannot be explained, it can, up to a point, be expressed, and this expression is the basis of the arts. The role of art, then, is primarily to express the complex of human existence, humanity's awareness of being itself rather than its perception of what is not itself and is outside it. This self-awareness is neither subjective nor objective, for man in himself is both an individual and, no less essentially, a member of the society which is partly inside him; and it is neither rational nor irrational. It does not quantify existence like science: it qualifies it: it tries to express, not what is there, but what is here, what is involved in consciousness and being themselves. The arts, then, belong to the phase of experience that we have learned to call existential, to an awareness that cannot be external to itself nor have anything external to it.

The production of art is, of course, a stylizing of behavior like the production of science. As far as the actual man doing the work is concerned, I doubt whether there is any essential psychological difference between the artist and the scientist, any "creative" factors present in one that are not present in the other. Both have to use the entire mind; both have much the same difficulties in getting that very complicated machine to work. But when we consider the finished product only, it is clear that the arts do not stabilize the subject in the same way that science does. Emotions, repressed or mythopoeic elements in the subconscious, the manipulating of data, the summoning up of controlled hallucinations (as expressed in the traditional phrase about poetry, *ut pictura poesis*), all have a function in the creation of art. The stabilized subject of science is usually identified with the reason; the unstabilized subject is normally called the imagination. The individual artist is a representative of human imagination, just as the individual scientist is a representative of human reason. But at no point, qua artist, is he outside the human world we call culture or civilization, just as the physical scientist, qua physical scientist studying "nature," is never inside it.

I speak of course of the arts in the plural because there is a group of them: music, literature, painting, sculpture, architecture, perhaps others. The dance, for instance, is in practice a separate art, though in theory it is difficult to see it as anything but a form of musical expression. It seems inherently unlikely, at the time of writing, that we have yet to develop a new art, despite all the strenuous experiment that there has been, some of it in that direction. Marshall McLuhan says of the new media of communication that "the medium is the message," and that the content of each medium is the form of another one. This surely means, if I understand it correctly, that each medium is a distinctive art. Thus the "message" of sculpture is the medium of sculpture, distinct from the message which is the medium of painting. But, as McLuhan also emphasizes, the new media are extensions of the human body, of what we already do with our eyes and ears and throats and hands. Hence they have given us new forms of variations of the arts we now have, and the novelty of these forms constitutes a major imaginative revolution in our time. But though distinctive arts they are not actually new arts: they are new techniques for receiving the impression of words and pictures.

Of these arts, literature is the art of words, and words are also the medium for the humanities and much of the sciences. This suggests that the arts, besides being arts, may also be informing languages for other disciplines. A painting or a poem is a construct: you look first of all at the associative factors in it, the things that make it hold together. But besides having paintings we have pictures of things: that is, there are things outside painting that we understand pictorially. For centuries philosophers expressed themselves in words, taking words for granted, forgetting that there is an art of words, not realizing that the verbal basis of philosophy constitutes a philosophical problem in itself. It seems to have been only in our own time that philosophers and logicians have really tried to become aware of the limitations of form (as distinct from the mere pitfalls or fallacies) inherent in the use of words. Even now their interest seems to be mainly linguistic rather than properly literary, and some philosophers are so ignorant of the source of their own subject that they regularly use "literary" in a pejorative sense. It is obvious that words lend themselves very readily to being an informing language for a descriptive discipline. Literature was not, up until the Romantic movement at least, regarded as the most impressive thing man does with words, the more objectified structures of theology and philosophy being regarded as higher in status and coming closer to what this conference calls the quest for truth. As compared with music, or even painting, there is always some reference to the outer world implicit in every use of words. Even if in the future we leave painting to the chimpanzees and music to chance, I do not see how literature can ever lose its kernel of externalizable meaning. And yet the capacity of words for informing other disciplines is not unlimited. Compared with mathematics at least, words are incurably associative: multiple meanings lurk in them and the structures of grammar twist them into nonrepresentational forms. It seems more likely that words have a certain radius of descriptive power, and that it is important to determine the approximate limits of that radius.

The other arts seem to differ widely in their powers of being able to inform other studies. Painting and sculpture, like literature, can be employed to represent the external world, and, again like literature, their descriptive or representational aspect has had more prestige in the past than their associative or constructive aspect. We can understand what their informing capacity is if we think not only of painting but of the pictorial arts, including illustrations, sketches, blueprints, diagrams, and models, and not only of sculpture but of the sculptural arts, including three-dimensional models. Some modern painters and sculptors, such as Miro or Giacometti, indicate the inherent relation of their arts with diagram and model very clearly. In some areas, such as geometry, the pictorial and the mathematical overlap, and of course the role of diagram in the sciences, as in the structural formulas of chemistry, is of immense importance. The question of whether light consists of waves or particles is surely, to some extent, a picturing problem. In my *Anatomy of Criticism* I have raised the question of the role of diagram in verbal thought as well. But to what extent and in what ways the pictorial and sculptural arts inform the humanities and sciences I do not know, nor have I read anybody who did know.

Music, on the other hand, has often been said to be the existential art par excellence, the hieratic, self-enclosed expression of pure being with no relation to an externalized order of any kind. Perhaps this is because it is, as Mrs. Langer suggests, the art of "virtual time," the closest expression of the continuous awareness of being which is the core of nonscientific experience. Or perhaps it is only because, up to the rise of electronic music, the music we know has been founded on a set of conventions as arbitrary as chess. On my piano as I write this is a sonata of Clementi called "Didone Abbandonata": we are supposed to think of the story of Dido while we listen. The finale is a rondo beginning with what for Clementi is a sharp discord, a minor ninth, and the movement is hopefully marked "con disperazione." But it soon collapses into the ordinary rondo structure, and by the time we reach the second subject it is clear that poor Dido has been abandoned once more. A greater composer would have been more tactful or created a more compelling musical mood: that is why the mediocre example illustrates more clearly my point, which is that music is not an informing art: it sets up a powerful centripetal force that resists being drawn into the structure of anything outside itself. We do use metaphors from music a good deal ("harmony," "overtones," and the like), and the old fables about the music of the spheres suggest that music may have an unsuspected informing power about it. Perhaps the myth of heaven as a place where harp playing is a compulsory cultural accomplishment will come true, and the theology and metaphysics of the future will be understood musically rather than verbally. When I read or try to read Heidegger I get the same feeling that I get when trying to read *Finnegans Wake,* of language dissolving into a mass of associative puns, and language of this kind is surely heading in the direction indicated by the squeals and groans of electronic music.

If words can be used both to construct an art and to inform some of the descriptive disciplines, there seems no reason why we should not think of mathematics, which informs so much of the physical sciences, as an art too. It is a self-contained construct like the arts, and I do not see how it is possible to frame a definition, or even a description, of the arts that would include the five I have listed and exclude mathematics. But mathematics is the art of numerical or quantitative relationships, and so it has a unique capacity for giving order and coherence to the sciences, of providing their description and experiments with the repeatable element of law. In contrast to the other arts, it stabilizes the subject on the "rational" level, as science does, and is so constantly informing the physical sciences that it is often regarded as simply a part of them. Hence some of the more speculatively-minded scientists and philosophers are occasionally surprised to discover that nature has a mathematical form. Of course it has: they put it there. And because it informs science

44

so readily, mathematics practised as an art in its own right is a rare and esoteric achievement, though its tradition can be traced from the semioccult use of it associated with the name of Pythagoras down to the later work of Einstein.

The rise of modern science involved a new way of looking at the external world which is most lucidly set out in Locke, though it had been there at least since Galileo. According to this the world has secondary qualities which are experienced by sensation, and primary qualities independent of such experience, which can only be weighed and measured. This distinction has a rough but significant analogy to the role of words in rendering the external world as compared with the role of mathematics. Mathematics is the language that can render the world of primary qualities: words never lose their connexion with human action and human sensation on which the two primary categories of words, verbs and nouns, are based. To the extent that an electron, for instance, is given a name and made a noun, it becomes a potential object of perception, unlikely as it is that it will ever be an actual one. The radius of verbal information, then, apparently runs between the human body and its environment as perceived and experienced by that body. The nonliterary function of words is thus, in the broad Kantian sense, critical: words can be used to explain the human situation, instead of merely expressing it as literature does, but they always remain connected with that situation.

The conception of science, as a systematic understanding of nature under law for which the appropriate language is mathematics, is of course a relatively recent one. For thousands of years before the great scientific explosion of the last few centuries, thinkers had been making constructs of the outer world, mainly verbal and pictorial. In these constructs the associative characteristics of the arts from which they were derived are very obvious. Poets find it much easier to live in the Ptolemaic universe than in ours, because it is more associative; modern poets turn from science to occultism because the latter still features associative patterns. Very early the two great containing conceptions of the scientific attitude made their appearance: "substance," or the objectified world visible and invisible, and "soul," the ideally disembodied intelligence which contemplates it. These parents then peopled the world with various offspring, ideas, essences, universals, atoms, and the like. The great difficulty with using words, when attempting to deal with primary qualities, is the readiness with which words adapt themselves to what we may call, altering Whitehead's phrase, pseudoconcreteness. Adam named the animals because he could see them, but, as Theseus says in Shakespeare, it is just as easy to name airy nothings, to bestow nouns on and make verbal objects out of things that are not there, or cannot be proved to be there. Again, the prestige of the subject-object relationship meant that attempts to express what is genuinely existential, the human situation itself, could take the form of the *metaphorically* objective. The conception of a spiritual world is a metaphorical verbal object of this kind. With the rise of modern science, words have become more limited in their range. Metaphysics seemed for a time to be taking the form of a verbalized general science, expressing for its age some sense of what scientific activity as a whole is doing. It is more at home however with the assumptions on which scientific work is based, because those assumptions are part of the human context of science, and so they can be dealt with critically, which means verbally.

The principle of a metaphorical object is of central importance when we try to see what the place of content is in the arts. The activity of consciousness, of externalizing reality, is always part of the whole existential com-

46

plex. The aspect of painting that reproduces or "imitates" an outer world exists in painting as, so to speak, a metaphor of externality. Even music has, in the witty and paradoxical form of "programme" music, a metaphorical external world of this kind, and literature has it in everything that we call realism. We are constantly using quantitative expressions (e.g., "I love you very much") as metaphors for things that are not quantities. Aristotle, who approached the arts for a scientific point of view (one of his most illuminating comments on art is in the *Physics*), spoke of the arts as imitative of nature. But as soon as we examine this conception of imitation, the notion of a continuous relation to the external world begins to dissolve, and we can see that "nature" exists in art only as the content of art, as something that art surrounds and contains. So while science deals with the consolidating of what is there, the arts deal with the expanding of what is here; the circumference of science is the universe, the circumference of the arts is human culture. In our time the sense of cleavage between the expression of what is here and the study of what is there is very sharp. We tend to feel that whatever is objective or external belongs only to the spatial world of science: every other "there" is a metaphor derived from that spatial world, and such metaphors no longer carry much conviction. Theology, for example, or at least the Protestant versions of it that I am more familiar with, is now trying to come to terms with the fact that nothing it is talking about is actually "there." God is certainly not "there": he has been deprived of all scientific function and he has no status in the spatial world of science, including the temporal world that can be divided and measured. So whatever the present or future of theology may be, it cannot be the queen of sciences as we now think of science: science deals only with It, and can take no part in an I-Thou dialogue.

47

For a long time, of course, it was assumed that the study of nature was also the study of a revelation of God, the order and coherence of nature being assumed to be the result of divine design. This view was contemporary with the view that the models of human civilization themselves, the city and the garden, were also of divine origin. But just as man came finally to believe that he had created and was responsible for his own civilization, so he came also to believe that the real basis of science was the correspondence of nature and human reason. Whatever is there in nature, the mind can find something in verbal or mathematical reasoning that will explain, assimilate or inform it. "The external world is fitted to the mind," as Wordsworth says. So although nature is an externalized reality, it is not, for science, an alien one. In fact science, as a form of knowledge, could even be thought of as a gigantic human narcissism, the reason falling in love with its own reflexion in nature. Whenever there have been antiscientific trends in human culture, they have usually seized on some aspect of this principle, though their target has been less science itself than the kind of essential philosophy that preceded it. Existentialism, for example, insists that if we think of the external world as a human world, certain elements become primary that are carefully kept out of science: the imminence of death, the feeling of alienation, the pervading sense of accident and of emptiness, and the direct confrontation with something arbitrary and absurd. Once we take away from externality the rational structure that we have put into it, it becomes what Milton calls a universal blank. All science is founded on the equation A equals B, where A is the human reason and B the rationally comprehensible element in nature. The existentialists may be described as the people who have discovered that if A equals B, then A minus B equals nothing.

48

We notice that existentialists have some difficulty in making their philosophy self-sufficient. Most of the best of them have incorporated it into a religious attitude, and of the atheistic ones, Heidegger went along with the Nazis and Sartre has recently collapsed on the bosom of the Church Marxist. It looks as though the attitude, along with whatever antiscientific bias it may have, belongs in a larger context which is normally either religious or revolutionary, or both. That larger context is a view, found in very different forms in Blake, Kierkegaard, Nietzsche and D. H. Lawrence, which might be paraphrased somewhat as follows:

Reality is primarily what we create, not what we contemplate. It is more important to know how to construct a human world than to know how to study a nonhuman one. Science and philosophy are significant as two of the creative things that man does, not as keys to the reality of the world out there. There is a world out there, but science sees it as a world under law, and no vision under law can ever give us the whole truth about anything. Science moves with greatest confidence, and makes its most startling discoveries, in a mechanical and unconscious world. If we remove science from its context and make it not a mental construct but an oracle of reality, the logical conclusion is that man ought to adjust himself to that reality on its terms. Thus moral law imitates natural law, and human life takes on the predictable characteristics of nature as science reveals it. What begins as reason ends in the conditioned reflexes of an insect state, where human beings have become cerebral automata. The real world, that is, the human world, has constantly to be created, and the one model on which we must not create it is that of the world out there. The world out there has no human values, hence we should think of it primarily not as real but as absurd. The existential paradoxes help us to do

49

this, and they thereby reduce the world to the *tohu-wa-bohu,* the waste and void chaos of a world which man has once again to create.

In science applied to the human world, that is, in applied science and technology, we see the mathematical shape of science itself, from the pyramids of Egypt and the highways and aqueducts of Rome to the chessboard cities and cloverleaf intersections of our day. For Blake, and in some degree for Lawrence, these mathematical shapes in human life are symbols of aggression: human life is at its most mathematical and automatic in military operations, and in Blake the pyramid, and more particularly the "Druid" trilithon, the ancestor of the Roman arch, are symbols of imperialistic hysteria and malevolence. Every advance in technology is likely to cause an immense legal complication in life, as the automobile has done, and the sheeplike panic-stricken stampeding of modern life, of which the totalitarian state is a by-product, is part of a technological way of life. Popular fiction has been exploiting the figure of the mad scientist for over a century, and there really does seem to be such a thing as mad science: psychology used to enslave people, nuclear physics used to exterminate the human race, microbiology suggesting even more lethal methods of trying to improve it. However, even in their most antiscientific pronouncements such writers as Blake and Lawrence seldom if ever say that science is the direct cause of the sinister will to slavery in modern times. They say rather that man has lost his nerve about taking charge of his own world, through a false theory of knowledge in which he is "idolatrous to his own shadow," as Blake says, and that this loss of nerve expresses itself as a perversion and parody of science. The world out there is real, but if we *deify* its reality, if we make it an object of imitation, it takes on the outlines of Satan the accuser, belittling us with its vast size in time and space, contemptuous of our efforts to be free of its colossal machinery.

The contrast I am paraphrasing is more conventionally phrased in other writers, and is often put into the form of an antithesis between values and facts. But the word value still has something prefabricated about it, a suggestion of something immutable laid up in a Platonic heaven. It is man's right to create his world that must be safeguarded, and every creation is likely to require a transvaluation of the past. Besides, values are really for the most part still forms of law, and do not get us out of our dilemma. The same is true of the moral categories of Kierkegaard, the "ethical freedom" of the man who has passed beyond speculation. It would be better to use the existential terms engagement or concern to express the contrast between a reality which is there to begin with and the greater reality which, like religious faith or artistic creation, does not exist at all to begin with, but is brought into being through a certain kind of human act.

Science is increasingly a communal and corporate activity. The humanities are more individualized, and the arts are intensely so: schools and isms in the arts are a sign of youth and immaturity, of an authority not yet established in the single artist. When we think of the scientist as voyaging through strange seas of thought alone, as Wordsworth did Newton, we are probably thinking of him primarily as a mathematician. We are, in contrast to Communist countries, extremely permissive about a writer's loneliness: we allow our writers to retire into what sometimes seem very neurotic fairylands, because they may also be areas of the unstabilized imaginative vision. The result is that communication in and from the arts is a slow and cumbersome business, and that is why we need the dimension of criticism, the vision of artists as a society engaged in a communal enterprise.

51

As soon as we take this critical perspective on literature, we see that literature is organized by huge containing conceptions which establish the literary societies and the family resemblances among large groups of writers. We call these containing forms myths, and it is in these myths that the nature of man's concern for his world is most clearly expressed. Our own age expresses itself chiefly in the ironic myth, and irony marks the ascendance of a technological society and the tendency of man to imitate the natural law outside him. It is in the ironic mode that the writer deals with the human situation as though it were external to him and as though he were detached from it, and in this mode that he sees human behavior as mechanized, frustrated, and absurd. If one were to say to almost any serious contemporary writer: "But I don't like the characters and situations you present to me," he would almost certainly answer: "That's because I'm trying to tell the truth as I see it." In our day the writer defends himself in language parallel to the language of science and other objective disciplines. These myths also inform the structures built out of words that exist outside literature, that is, in general, the humanities. Existentialism, with its conceptions of anguish, nausea, and the like, is an ironic philosophy, a fact which accounts for the lack of self-sufficiency I spoke of before. Irony, in literature, is a sophisticated myth, best understood as a frustration or parody of the more primitive comic and romantic myths in which a quest is successfully accomplished. These romantic and comic myths are those that inform Christianity and the revolutionary myth of Marxism. Earlier in this paper I quoted from Freud's *Future of an Illusion*. Religion was a subject Freud had a Freudian block about, mainly because he wanted to be a lawgiving Moses in his own right, contemplating the back parts of his own God. As a literary critic, I am interested in the fact that Freud and Marx are the two most influential thinkers in the world today, that both of them developed an encyclopaedic programme that they called scientific, and that nine-tenths of the science of both turns out to be applied mythology. These mythical expressions of concern, in which man expresses his own attitude to the culture he has built, are subject to a disease of thinking which is best called anxiety, in the Freudian and not the existential sense. We often find that those who are committed to a religious or revolutionary faith have a peculiar difficulty in being intellectually honest in their arguments: their commitment wants to twist and manipulate facts, to maintain tendentious lines of reasoning, to rationalize or simply assert things for which there is no evidence. The record of Christianity is full of persecutions in the name of absurdities, and Marxism is also an anxiety structure, with a sensitive nose for heresies and deviations. The reason for this kind of anxiety is, again, a failure of nerve, a refusal to accept the fact that man continually creates his world anew, a desire to have it fit something outside itself. What is outside, in this sense, cannot be in space: it can only be in time, a pattern established in the past, or to be established in the future, to which all facts and discoveries somehow must be adjusted.

In the sciences it is possible to carry on one's studies with an undeveloped sense of concern. There are scientists who irritably brush off the suggestion that what they are doing may have momentous consequences for good or evil, and that they should be concerned for those consequences. A sense of concern would make such a scientist more presentable as a human being: it would also unite him to the community he lives in, and work against the dehumanizing tendency inherent in all specialization. There is no way of overcoming the barriers of specialization, no way of making a Romance philologist and a solid-state physicist intellectually intelligible to each other. But they are united by being both citizens of their society, and their realization of this makes both Romance philology and solid-state physics liberal arts, studies that liberate mankind. In science this social concern affects the scientist as man, but not so much qua scientist. But in the humanities the great poetic myths are also shaping forms: in history, in philosophy, in criticism, a scientific detachment and a humane engagement are fighting each other like Jacob and his angel. That is why the humanities are difficult to characterize, not only in methodology, but even as a distinctive group of studies in themselves.

To sum up, then: it does not seem to me that the really important difference between the humanities and the sciences is in the difference in their subject matter. It is rather that science exhibits a method and a mental attitude, most clearly in the physical sciences, of a stabilized subject and an impartial and detached treatment of evidence which is essential to all serious work in all fields. The humanities, on the other hand, express in their containing forms, or myths, the nature of the human involvement with the human world, which is essential to any serious man's attitude to life. As long as man lives in the world, he will need the perspective and attitude of the scientist; but to the extent that he has created the world he lives in, feels responsible for it and has a concern for its destiny, which is also his own destiny, he will need the perspective and attitude of the humanist.

THE UNIVERSITY AND THE LITERARY PUBLIC

By FRANK KERMODE

WHEN A UNIVERSITY reaches the age of one hundred years it is as wise as it will ever be. It has acquired a real knowledge of how knowledge changes. It knows the secrets not only of learning, but of unlearning. Its faculty has experienced the full taste of mortality and at the same time come to understand the nature of its immortality as *persona ficta*. It is conversant with other immortal persons, with the perpetuity of the exigent young, who nevertheless pass on quadrennially. It is wise, in short, because it has acquired over its century an instinctive understanding of continuity and change.

The hundred years of this university have been unusually copious in the provision of lessons on change. To have been born in the year when the Civil War ended; to have come in with antiseptics; to have as one's coevals not only *Drum Taps* but *War and Peace,* is to have a congenital association with ends and beginnings, with crisis. Did anyone at Lexington consider what it meant to open a university at a time when an Oxford don was writing a post-Euclidian and pre-Freudian book *for children?* For 1865 is the date of *Alice in Wonderland.* Did some humanist, weltering in the chaos of a newly opened Admissions office, console himself with the thought that Kentucky had arranged a handsome six-hundredth birthday offering to Dante? I hope so; for there is a sense in which he would not merely have been cheering himself up but speaking the truth. He would have been expressing the same apprehension of essential continuity that has prompted the University, in its unchallengeable wisdom, to celebrate its centennial with, among other deliberations more likely to change the world, a conference on the Humanities, which change only men.

You will observe that I have gone in for some "centurial mysticism," as Henri Focillon called it; but I can hardly be criticized for doing that by an audience whose coming together expresses a unanimous approval of the same superstition. But of course it is not superstition but simple commonsense to assert, by whatever means, the association of the university with men and works such as those I named. They are great men and great works because universities exist; they survive because universities exist. If Dante walked in Oxford he walked also in Lexington. You will perhaps be remembering Max Beerbohm's drawing which shows the terrifying poet looking reflectively down upon a pompous proctor and his bulldogs. But though he might have difficulty understanding the administration, he would have none in seeing that what the scholars, senior and junior, were doing or trying to do, was essentially and intimately his business.

I have abandoned *Drum Taps* and *Alice in Wonderland* in favor of Dante, and I will explain why. There are two topics I want, on this occasion, to talk about. One of them is our critical duty, broadly conceived, in the humanistic faculties. The other, which has logical priority though in practice it is inseparable from the first, is the role of the university in the perpetuation of a literary public. And in discharging this second duty the university is obviously doing Dante's work.

I shall be saying that our critical duty has to do, to a great extent, with change; but we have this prior duty in respect of a literary public, and that duty is best understood in terms of continuity. Of course the distinction I am making is, for dialectical purposes, deliberately exaggerated. Nevertheless, we all know that whereas a humanistic training tends to develop in us (that is, in the senior members of the university) a habit of attention to the past, the world, and a more active biology, commit us (especially the junior members of the university) to change and the future. We also know that from generation to generation we change the past; that is why I said universities learn not only to learn but to unlearn. As the generations shorten and grow more mobile, the gap between them widens; and there has of late been striking evidence that senior and junior, within the university, see the world as well as the past in different ways. Thus the university contains members who verge on abolitionism, as Professor Barzun calls it, and others who are traditionalist: *passéistes* and *anti-passéistes*, if you can stand the terms.

Now it is useless to argue that the university must be one or the other. It cannot be *anti-passéiste*, simply because it is what it is; but it cannot be entirely *passéiste* either, or, like Stevens' general, it will look rigid and a bit absurd. Just as it accommodates different generations, it has to reconcile their views. It has to ensure that the right lessons are learned, and the right lessons unlearned. In short, it has to convince its junior members of the use of the past and the indispensability of continuity. If it is a university at all, it has to work in such a way that it will seem natural, on its two-hundredth birthday, and on the eight-hundredth birthday of Dante, to hold a humanities conference which will discuss not only the past but the crisis of learning; for the one thing we can confidently predict is that there will be a crisis of learning. It follows from the nature of the world, and from the difference between being and knowing. Now if that conference occurs it will be a proof that something started by Dante is still going on. It will mean that the university has done

one of its jobs, its basic humanistic job, which is to perpetuate the literary public.

What is a literary public? We should know, for it is what we try to produce or maintain in our undergraduate schools. And though some of us may feel a twinge of guilt at the thought, that is where our most important work lies. Historians nowadays sometimes speak of a kind of European apocalypse, of a culture "nearing its term"; in fact this is the expression of Erich Auerbach, who did so much to define what is meant by a literary public. Now it seems that the graduate schools might survive this sad event. There one speaks a learned language; but the business of the undergraduate school is conducted in the vernacular. The learning of the Carolingian schools was conducted in Latin, and there was no learning outside them for lack of an adequate vernacular. The same difficulty threatened early Renaissance humanism. The creation and maintenance of a literary public requires the creation and maintenance of an adequate high vernacular. Dante created it, and our business is to maintain it. Of course our graduate students are saved from inverted barbarism, as it were, by having been through a course of vernacular instruction, and their more advanced work is to acquire the means by which one asks the right questions of the past, and the means by which to estimate, for the benefit of the next generation, the quality of contemporary efforts at finding things out by humanistic study. It is important work, but without the vernacular studies of the undergraduate nobody could be trained to do it, and there would be nobody to do it for.

The creation of a high vernacular, to which we can give the "ideal date" of 1300, established a literary public. And this made possible a developing, changing literature of the modern sort. The forms of literature, as of art, depend

58

for their effect upon a collaboration between artist and public. It is a point made beautifully clear, so far as painting is concerned, by E. H. Gombrich. It has not been so expressly stated for literature, yet the situation is analogous. Without a communications agreement founded on this vernacular, this *vulgaris nobilior,* literature could not have invented for itself new conventions, new fields of interest. There could not have been that history of increasingly sophisticated means, careful archaistic reversions, new forms creating the taste by which they were to be enjoyed. There could not even have been the literature which rebels against the literary language or the literary public, since the nature and extent of the rebellion can only be measured if you speak the language or understand the assumptions of the public rejected. And that is why I say that our first task is simply to teach this language.

The job is partly a historian's job, but by no means entirely so. It is also partly a matter of inducing acceptance of much that may seem arbitrary, by whatever means one can. More and more, we may find, the young resist the proposition that they cannot know any literature, even the book that came out today, without learning something of the language we teach. Often the complaint of the undergraduate is quite justified; he can complain, so to speak, that he asks for Dante's vernacular and we give him Carolingian Latin. He can say we have forgotten that the present is what determines the interest of the past, and that he has no wish to belong to the company of, or speak the language of, a dead reading public. But we are all so timid about the young just now, so afraid to seem to put ourselves against them—an aspect of that cultural complacency rightly said by Diana Trilling to be just as bad as anticultural complacency—that it's necessary here to add that the complaint of the undergraduate is also often unjustified. He has his rights, but so has the immortal *persona ficta,* the reading public. Nobody is literary on instinct; it has to be learned.

It may well be that the way to teach the young what they need to know in order to join this august body is not what it used to be. P. B. Medawar has recently been ridiculing what he calls Anglo-Saxon attitudes to scientific research. The scientist, we say, is concerned with the growth of organized factual knowledge, but the burden of facts is becoming insupportable, and so everybody retreats into minute specialisation, and communications, even between scisntists engaged in different branches of one subject, say physics, break down. And much more of the same kind of thing. Medawar calls this "false in every particular," and declares that the thoughts he has been criticising are "not really thoughts at all, but thought-substitutes, declarations of the kind public people make on public occasions when they are desperately hard up for something to say." The need to learn facts, in zoology for instance, is less than it was a hundred years ago; modern science has seen the breakdown of specialisms; and so on. Everything depends upon the criteria by which knowledge is valued. In literature there was a notion that the study of modern as apposed to ancient literature could provide the discipline formerly associated with difficult languages and remote history. So the emphasis fell on the learning of facts. We are following the sciences out of this phase. As Medawar puts it, the scientist values what he is doing by the size of its contribution to a logically articulated structure of ideas; the humanist has been a nuisance in a way because he has a deep distrust of utility, and cannot see, as scientists can, that it is compatible with "elegance" and "beauty"; nevertheless he must come to value his work by the contribution it makes "directly or indirectly, to our understanding of human nature and conduct, and human sensibility."

I'll return to the comparison with science; meanwhile the point is that Medawar is right about the humanities, and this being so we must relate our methods of teaching the *volgare illustre* to such aims as he—a little vaguely, perhaps, but the point isn't central to his argument—lays down. This way of estimating the value of instruction in the humanities is acceptable to the student, though he may not like some of the disciplines involved; they may strike him as having little to do with his world. It is no use denying, given the social constitution of a university, that this is the primary problem: teaching the lesson of continuity to intelligent people who are sceptical about its relevance. How, in the wisdom of a hundred years, will a university deal with it?

First, by recognising the force of change. The needs of the student *are* different. The past of literature *has* changed; we must be sure that the image we have of it is not eidetic, that we have not accepted a receipt to deceive. Secondly, and more positively, by establishing a fertile relationship between the two broadly conflicting attitudes that come together whenever we sit with an undergraduate. This we can only do by a sort of symbiotic process, made possible by the presence of the book or topic we happen to be discussing. The aim, as I see it, must be to enable the student to read with what Michael Polanyi calls "tacit intelligence." Polanyi's illustration of this attribute is from the sciences, naturally enough; but one of the reasons why we should value him highly is that he will not allow that there is, in respect of the way the mind is used, any generic difference between the most authentic activities of science and the humanities. "Tacit" intelligence enables a doctor to make a diagnosis or a critic to understand a poem. It would not be possible to specify the mental acts and decisions involved in such acts; they are the effect of powers the knower has acquired, and they are essential to any kind of knowing that gives the knower the satisfaction of truth or beauty or elegance, or whatever you care to call the feeling that one knows, whether what is understood is called a problem in physics or a poem. Polanyi argues that this implies in all knowledge an inescapable degree of personal participation.

Scientists are, indeed, much franker about this situation than critics. They know how Newton and Einstein and Planck can all be relevant, and speak freely of "elegance." Of course, I do not propose that in our business of teaching a language and forming a literary public we should revert to ejaculatory criticism; by "elegant" a scientist means complete, economical, achieved, and usually, by some easy implication, useful. Speaking thus of "Resolution and Independence" for instance, is unlikely to impress a sceptical undergraduate, who might well argue that it is, as he understands the words, inelegant, clumsy in fact. Its text is not, like a theorem or the report of an experiment, self-explanatory. You might reply by suggesting that there are reasons, in tradition, in rhetoric, in Wordsworth's earlier poems, for this one having such a shape, and making such demands. But this would be an attempt to relate it to some systematic description of literature in something like the way the new hypothesis of the physicist is related to the logical structure of science in general. The student might reply, "Ortega was right, it seems, about the dehumanisation of art, and the curious thing is that it should happen at the very time when the scientists were giving up their pretensions to inhumanity." If you still want to make of him a man who will tacitly recognise that "Resolution and Independence" is a great poem you must do more than talk about the history of poetry, or the history of ideas, or the occult mythic structure of literature; you must bully him into a personal participation in this piece of knowledge: explain for instance, that the apparent inelegance, translated into the high vernacular, is the ultimate elegance. The *turpiloquium* of the old man is caught up in a cardinal language, a new extension of the *volgare illustre*. Now this is hard work, a rhetorical performance however small the scale. But when you have done it you have the pleasure of knowing that something has happened—the encounter of a mind with something to be known that changes the mind for good —which will never be undone. The poem will never be a mere object again. It is almost a union of two persons— "weak minds on love revealed may look." The mind and sensibility so affected has a more effective store of tacit knowledge to bring to the next encounter.

Ideally, when he graduates, this young man will need you no more, and may even, unless he teaches himself, wonder why you made such a fuss about something so obvious. He knows, without working it out explicitly, what marvellous feats of counterpointing, what intricacies of peripeteia, what intellectual shocks, are concealed in "Resolution and Independence." He will bring this knowledge to *King Lear,* or *War and Peace* or *Drum Taps,* or to *An American Dream* and *Kaddish.* And he will not merely participate, he will judge. The knowledge he has acquired of the way things mean more or other than they say, and that their meanings change by his own intervention, will serve him outside literature; for in such respects the literary public is only the acutest point of the whole culture, and in every department ours has been and is a culture which assumes that things mean more or other than they say. If you suggest that the example I gave is an instance of brainwashing, I accept the charge; nobody with a perfectly open mind ever became a Christian, a poet, a philosopher, a historian, or a critic. And it is worth noting, as Wallace Stevens liked to point out, that the gods of China are always Chinese and that Danes are happiest in Denmark. In short, what you call brainwashing I call acquiring a tacit knowledge of the peculiar assumptions and conditions of one's own cultural tradition.

I have now to admit that the undergraduate endowed with such knowledge is a rare specimen. What he did was to learn from the teacher how to engage a prepared mind with a work of art belonging to the order we elect to call the highest. It is too cosy a story, as we all know. There arise the questions, whether instead of this random propaganda and desperate intuition we cannot have a more systematic approach to literary study; and whether all this doesn't beg the undergraduate's question, since it assumes continuity where he assumes schism. I find both of these questions to be serious and complicated, and instead of trying to answer them directly I shall turn to what I announced as the second of the topics I should touch on in this talk; what I called non-committally, our critical duty.

First of all, we must take the young man seriously and attend, though this means a deviation from the natural and easier bent of our attention, to change. Like the giant in the poem, the university must live in change, as the high vernacular also lives in change:

> . . . l'uso di mortali è come fronda
> in ramo, che sen va e altra vene.
> (*Paradiso* xxvi, 137-8)

"The usage of mortals is like a leaf on a branch, which goes and another comes."

In other words, it does not seem to me to be part of our critical duty to argue, with our superior skill, for an unchallengeable order of literature upon which the sempiternal literary public must pasture, without in some measure undertaking to justify that order as relevant to a modern sense of reality. *King Lear,* I am quite certain, is a good play; and I am certain of more, namely that anybody who does not *know* this is unlikely to say much of any interest about plays, or poems, or history, or perhaps anything. Nevertheless, it is arguable that *King Lear* is a disordered and even ignorant document; that it lacks "elegance"; that, like the language of the Romans with which straight roads were built, it *was* good but had to die. A good undergraduate might argue thus, or rather argue better; he might say that *Malone Dies* or *Howl* was for him a better instrument with which to find out the unknown things about oneself for which *King Lear* was formerly an acceptable instrument of search. For an epoch, as Einstein said, is the instruments of its research. How do we explain that tacit knowledge which accepts that *Lear,* the instrument of an earlier epoch, still works, and that *Malone Dies* would be reduced to impotence by the same stroke that disabled *Lear?*

This defense of *Lear* seems in the long run to require that one say as clearly as possible what one conceives literary studies to be. Whatever one says must allow for changes, not only in what is studied but in the manner of study; this is the wisdom of a university. Thus there was a time when it was a tenable view that scientific history, or scientific classification, was the main or even the sole business of criticism. But why should we pretend that this remains true? Philosophers of history no longer accept the possibility of what used to be called scientific history—Ranke's "precisely what happened." Windelband, Rickert and Dilthey established what has been called "the secession of history from the natural sciences," though we need not call it that; Dilthey only said that the *Geisteswissenschaften* differed from the *Naturwissenschaften* in that they could be known from within. Windelband believed that history differed from the sciences because it dealt with events that were unique, whereas the natural

65

sciences are impossible except in relation to repeating or repeatable events. It may be that these distinctions are too sharp. If the direction of our interest were different we might read in the great achievements of scientific theory something equivalent to the confessional element in poetry, some experience of the world as unique as a poem, and as much the product of what Dilthey calls "living through" as a poem. But some distinctions nevertheless remain. Planck's constant is valuable, I take it, not because it cost him much mental pain and not only because it is "elegant" but because it works, even for those who haven't in any sense "lived through" it. It assumes repetitiveness in the nature of things, though it is indeed a very refined repetitiveness, calling for an extraordinary effort of imagination to formulate it. "Resolution and Independence," or *King Lear,* can be absolutely dead things, painfully produced no doubt; or they can, by straining the word, be called "elegant"; but they are not experiments you can invigilate; they are experiences correlative with the mental pains that produced them, experiences in which you participate, miming their elegances perhaps, tacitly repeating their questions even, but in no acceptable sense of the word using them, or, without entering them, checking their conformity with the experience of reality. And to place them in some flat pseudoscientific historic scale, or to classify them according to Linnaean schemes, however subtle, is to say nothing of them that is of any use to the people they chiefly concern, the literary public.

Long ago T. S. Eliot, among others, suggested that we should think of literature as having "a simultaneous existence" and composing a "simultaneous order." There is more than one way of regarding this famous proposition. Let me suggest two ways. One is Professor Frye's; his whole effort is really to make us see that our business is to describe this order. There is, I think, time in his universe, but it is not very important; all literature is produced by the displacement of certain radical themes which, if they are archaic, are also perpetual. The other I shall express for the moment by what may seem a difficult formula, which I shall explain in a minute. It suggests that the proposition is valid, and may be the base for valid inference, on the assumption that what it really implies is our power, by our tacit knowledge of the *volgare illustre,* to participate in past literature by treating it as a *special case* of our more immediate concerns. We can call the first of these Professor Frye's theory, and the second simply the special case theory.

Let me first say a word about Professor Frye's theory. It has power and elegance, but it pushes criticism back to the position history was in before Windelband's secession. If your aim is to assimilate any literary document with the ultimate categories of "undisplaced" myth it is obvious that your account of the work, however ingenious, is calculated to make it appear more like some other work which has to be got into the same category than it appeared before you began. Thus when you are speaking of Shakespeare's comedies you move back "from the characteristics of the individual play" to the consideration of "what kind of a form comedy is," and when you step back far enough you see a myth they have in common, as when it is argued that Andromeda is behind the heroines of the romances. The figure used by Mr. Frye is "stepping back," as you step back from a picture to see its formal design; but a better figure would be a slow putting out of the lights on the theory that all cats are grey in the dark. Mr. Frye would probably say that when I emphasise the uniqueness of great works of art, their challenge to personal participation, I am saying nothing particularly offensive or even that I am saying something banal; but he would also say that it has nothing whatever to do with criticism. This of course is what I deny. I don't, for example, imagine that he himself could have written a book so devoted to the avoidance of value judgments if he weren't habituated, as teachers are, to making them very unobtrusively, as he does in *Anatomy*. *Between the Acts,* he remarks in a casual aside, is Virginia Woolf's profoundest novel. I agree; but I claim the critic's right to say so.

One's protest, in fact, is all of a piece. If literature is radically spatial, unrelated to time, and changing only in a cycle of modes, it is certainly curious that we have such difficulty over critical terminology. We are still not sure what we mean when we use Aristotle's, which has been current since the beginnings of modern criticism; we are constantly in need of new terms to describe, not marginal changes or modal variations, but the most fundamental qualities of past literature. Time and literature change, we change with it. If we omit to consider this simple fact, and the related one that it changes at a different rate for the young, we substitute, in my earlier figure, Carolingian Latin for the *lingua franca et jocundissima*. Instead of the progressive and scientific system we were promised we get a monkish game.

It is possible that the argument I am constructing is too old or obvious to interest you much. I am saying that an undue attention to types and archetypes frustrates the act of personal participation which is the distinctive act of a literary public. To put it another way, in an expression borrowed from Sartre, who however uses it in philosophical and political contexts, dependence on eidetic imagery is an indication of *mauvaise foi*. I am not calling Professor Frye a *salaud,* though perhaps I am hinting that his regressive or eidetic theory of literature is a piece of cosmic toryism, a high mimetic approach to the topic which time and change must invalidate, and which can hardly serve the needs of our catechumens, the antibourgeois young.

68

I have been speaking of Mr. Frye, somewhat unfairly, as a representative, because he has in another and extremely interesting form the obsession with *scientific* philology from which *Scrutiny* and the New Criticism gave us a holiday lasting a quarter of a century. But I am not advocating a return either to the antiscience of the Symbolist criticism or to the a-methodical method of the *Scrutiny* critics, who certainly believed in personal participation but all too readily substituted a quasi-dogmatic apparatus of tradition and a bleak dissociationist sociology; if Frye looks like an angelologist they, at their dogmatic worst, sound like double predestinarians. What I do suggest is that we can hold a view of our critical duty which is consistent with the preservation of a literary public in a society more obviously able to cope with the intellectual structures of science. In outlining this view I shall be explaining what a few moments ago I called the special case theory of past literature.

To do that is not, I think, to set up some impassable barrier between science and literature; on the contrary, it will be necessary to argue that in their usefulness as ways of settling us into the world they are radically similar. Certainly science is about reality experienced as repetitive, and art about reality experienced as constituted of unique events; but that we do experience reality in both these ways is a fact about the way our minds work.

The scientists have become critical of their fictions, even though their metaphysic aims at regularity; they understand the readiness of nature to conform, and so interest themselves in concords rather than in absolute truth. Concords are humanly pleasing and consoling. In literary fictions we seek similarly consoling and pleasing concords, but as Blackmur once observed, our metaphysic has grown irregular. It is so because we also are much more critical of the truth-bearing function of fictions than we were; and this is true of historiographic as well as of literary-critical fictions; it is also true of novels, our predominant fictional form, where, so history tells us, the urge to be free of the paradigm is one of the ways in which we estimate greatness. It is our consciousness of the difficult status of fictions that prevents their achieving the sort of generality that pleases many and pleases long; they are quickly obsolescent, and a sense of reality as a paradigmatic is very strong in our time —especially, as I have been saying, in the young. All who teach the arts in universities would do well to remember what Matthew Arnold said of the way in which the satisfaction of our needs changes though our needs continue:

The Middle Age could do without humane letters, as it could do without the study of nature, because its supposed knowledge was made to engage the emotions so powerfully. Grant that the supposed knowledge disappears, its power of being made to engage our emotions will disappear with it,—but the emotions themselves, and their claim to be engaged and satisfied, will remain.

Nevertheless, everything I have said about the literary public and the high vernacular implies a defence of the paradigms. I believe, as practically everybody in our business except perhaps Leslie Fiedler believes, that they persist, that they are in fact inescapable. I distinguish here between what I call the paradigms—the radical patterns of fiction—and what are elsewhere called archetypes or myths. They may all be related in ways too deep for me; I should hope in fact that this is so, since harmony between dissident desires of the mind is what fictions provide; this is not quite the same thing as saying with Bacon that they submit the show of things to the desire of the mind, because one of our desires is to test our fictions by the elusive criterion of reality. Between the fictional paradigms and reality there is a gulf, the gulf of absurdity; at

70

worst we may feel that this is a model of the human condition. That is what Camus and Sartre said. A plot satisfies a need for causality, a peripeteia our sense that ends are predictable absolutely but not contingently, and so on; but all this is human, and it is also human to remind oneself occasionally that the world at large appears not to be like that. The peripeteia is part of *human* sentiment. When a plot is related not to reality but to some stereotype we are altogether too conscious of the absurdity; this is why Jane Austen rejected contemporary fiction and devised a new kind of novel, and why Henry James wrote "The Art of Fiction" and once again rethought the whole problem. Concords between fiction and reality are, in short, subject to decay. Literature inhabits time. Much of it seems to us absurd even when it is new; the rest of it, however humane, intelligent and complete its concords, is under a growing threat of absurdity. Is it then, like a scientific conjecture that experience or experiment refutes? What prevents us from discarding *King Lear*?

We are back at the catechumen's question. If you want to know "how it is" why not read *Comment c'est*? Isn't *Endgame* closer to our point than a story about early British ingratitude? In answering we must concede that though it is true, as Yeats remarked, that responsibilities begin in dreams, it is also true that we know the difference between a dream and a work of art, and that when Freud defined this as a matter of adjustment to reality he was saying what we all knew already; so that the rebellious student, as I said, has a right to this question. And yet a sense of the persistent relevance of *Lear* is obviously a condition of membership of the literary public. Note that *Lear* can be performed as a tragedy of the absurd; the argument is that in denying all absolutes Shakespeare turns tragedy into a farce of the sort that can be called grotesque or absurd, in a modern sense. Note also that *Endgame*

71

can be said to *include* Lear. Such is Kott's argument in his book on Shakespeare. Absurdity, he says, has replaced the absolute, but "the world of tragedy and the world of grotesque have a similar structure. Grotesque takes over the themes of tragedy and poses the same fundamental question."

I am not on the whole an admirer of this critic, but it seems to me that his absurdist redemption of *King Lear* is merely a somewhat exaggerated version of what, as accredited members of the literary public, we are all constantly engaged in. So long as certain structures survive we can accommodate the past, and when they no longer survive it will be time to stop talking about art. Physicists speak of classical Newtonian mechanics as a "special case" of quantum mechanics and so prevent a discontinuity of theory—they do not have to say that the probability doctrine works only for small quantum numbers, holding instead that when the quantum numbers are large—as they are in anything we normally experience—the situation is exactly the same but behaves *as if* Newtonian theory was right. So dodecaphonic musicians can regard diatonic music as a special case; and our catechumen may be encouraged to think of Shakespeare as playing Newton to Beckett's Heisenberg; the validity of *Lear* is maintained over practically the whole area of human experience. Its conformity with a changed reality, as well as its power to satisfy those needs we satisfy by means of fictions, are accordingly vindicated.

This is by no means a total answer to the charges brought by schismatics, but it does tell us what a large part of our critical office must be. It is to convince the postulant that if he learns the language and submits himself to the work he will discover its conformity with his own mind and the kinds of question he uniquely wants to ask. Even where it seems remote from his concerns, it has helped to shape those concerns, and so needs to be understood. We know so much more; precisely, as Eliot said: and the great works are that which we know. "We" in that formulation are the literary public.

Consequently I feel some irrelevance in arguments which stress the mythical basis as opposed to the heuristic function of great literature and the "scientific" as opposed to the more random "personalist" method. To make all literature rest scientifically on the great sunken foundations of a quest myth, or to satisfy oneself by relating it to its moment, seem to me ways of emphasising its potential of irrelevance. To say that its structure is in one way or another analogous to the structure of our own human enquiries into our condition you have to be prepared to relate it not to prehistoric or unconscious archetypes, but to the set of our own minds and to the codes still necessary to participation in art. In the past apocalypse absorbed prophecy, and tragedy absorbed apocalypse, and now perhaps tragedy has been absorbed by modes which allow for greater self-consciousness about fictions, and reduce the plight of the hero to absurdity; Sartre's existentialism does after all have a strongly tragic cast. It is the place of the older forms within our immediate concerns, their power to survive as formative for those concerns, that determines whether or no they do survive or can be revived. They live in change; if they cannot do so they are no longer susceptible to personal knowledge and they are relegated to the Latin schools.

Continuity, then, and the conclusion is not unfamiliar, is indispensable; what remains as the language of our *persona ficta,* the literary public, is what it could not function without. But of course it is we who uphold this continuity, and we can best do it by testing the works which constitute the high vernacular against the scepticism of those whose sense of reality diverges from ours. This is

73

done in universities, and in substitutes for and extensions of them. We may sometimes have to say no, in whatever kind of thunder we can muster, to the claims of some works to be included in the canon; some we take to be there we may have to expel. There has to be this dialogue between tradition and schism, between our acceptance and the fresh scepticism of the young. There is learning and unlearning; there is a controlled change in knowledge, but there is also the degree of perpetuity an institution can have. But everything I have said is part of the tacit knowledge of a university one hundred years old; which is why I began by saying that it is as wise as it will ever be because it can live in change, the tree which bears one generation and its language after another,

come fronda in ramo, che sen va e altra vene.

A JOURNALIST LOOKS AT
THE HUMANITIES

By BARRY BINGHAM

I FEEL THAT I should start this statement with an apology. There is a good deal of presumption in my appearing here to talk about the humanities among such eminent specialists as the other speakers at this Conference.

I come to you from the untidy field of journalism. The word "journalese" is not traditionally a term of flattery. At its best it is a synonym for hurried and superficial expression. At its most pejorative it is used to describe the cheap, the meretricious, and the vulgar. Many people in the academic world no doubt view the writing that is set before them in their daily newspaper in Milton's phrase: "The asinine feast of sow thistles and brambles."

There are four reasons, however, why I want to discuss the humanities with you from the standpoint of a working journalist. Let me summarize them:

1. I regard a good humanistic education as the best possible training for a newspaper career. Courses in the techniques of journalism can be helpful. The bedrock, however, is a sound training in the humanities.

2. I believe the arts and humanities will make more news in America in the next decade than in all the previous course of our history.

3. I consider the spread of humanistic education as the one hopeful escape for the American people from the besetting danger of an affluent society—the yawning emptiness that has been called "the abyss of leisure."

4. I am convinced that the humanities, teaching as

Professor Kermode says "the lesson of continuity," can help to supply standards for a society that is sick from the want of them.

To take my purely vocational point first, I always like to hire young men and women who have had a solid grounding in the liberal arts. Nothing so sharpens their power of observation and nothing so widens their gift of imagination. Newspaper work is far more demanding than it was a couple of generations ago. It used to be enough to hire a reporter who could rush out to cover a fire or an accident and come back with an accurate account of what happened. Those were the days of the old formula for a news story—who, what, when, where, and why. Such basic accuracy is still a requirement of the craft. In our times, however, a general assignments reporter may be asked to go out on successive days to interview a celebrated Russian composer, a nuclear physicist, and an expert in remedial reading. Every course he ever took in college may be called to his rescue at some point in his professional career.

Newspapers are coming to rely increasingly on reporting by specialists. They now operate in the fields of education, science, medicine, public welfare and city planning, as well as the older specialties of music, art and the theatre. Such specialists must obviously have sound training in the fields they undertake to cover. It is their job to write in such a way as to satisfy the professionals, while conveying a clear meaning of the material to the layman. This is no easy task. These specialists with basic courses in the humanities are a different breed from the hard-boiled, gum-snapping stereotype of the newspaperman who flourished in that classic of a past era called "The Front Page." Newspapers are turning increasingly to the best colleges to provide us with young recruits who can write good news material because they understand the basis of what they are writing about. That is the only kind of story that can give satisfaction to a reader. Such well-educated young journalists can help us to get rid of the hoary clichés of newspaper style. They can bring us closer to that clean simplicity of writing which makes the essays of Ralph Waldo Emerson, for all their elevation of thought, perfectly understandable to an eighth grade schoolboy. In many instances, let us hope, they may achieve Professor Kermode's "high vernacular."

On my second point, I believe the newspapers of America must prepare to report something like a cultural explosion in this country in the years just ahead. The New York *Times* has already advised us of the presence of a "culture industry." It notes that "consumer spending on the arts rose from 1953 to 1960 by about 130 percent, or considerably more than twice as fast as spending on all recreation, and better than six times as fast as the outlay for spectator sports." The *Times* analysis concludes with this comment: "We look for our society to become increasingly art-conscious at all levels. It would not surprise us to observe a major swing to conspicuous aesthetics." There is something a little disturbing in the way this thought is expressed. One is inclined to ask: If culture comes, can hucksterism be far behind? The resources of Madison Avenue are already devoted to the sale of certain items, such as book and record club memberships, on a basis of intellectual snobbery. There is nothing to regret, however, in the vast increase in the American sales of classical recordings, of good literature in paperback editions, and in original works of art. The newspapers must keep abreast of this national trend in their coverage of what is sometimes called "the culture beat." They must not only keep abreast but, to paraphrase Professor Kermode, even help bully our people into genuine participation in the knowledge which is art, history, philosophy, and literature. They must, as Professor Frye would say, help us to "qualify experience."

And this leads directly to my third point. It concerns the desperate need of the American people to find some constructive use for their increasing hours of leisure. No society in history has provided so much "spare time" away from the machine and the kitchen stove for so massive a portion of its people. The ruling classes of imperial Rome and of eighteenth century England enjoyed a set of privileges confined to a tiny minority of the population. We are now extending many of those privileges to the millions in America, and the process is inexorably spreading. It would be wicked to regard such an extension of leisure as anything but a glorious opportunity for a fuller, richer, more rewarding life. Yet there is a danger that leisure can become a burden in America instead of a blessing. To many it is a mere absence of occupation, a void that will begin to ache like a bad tooth if it is not quickly filled with some busy though meaningless activity.

If there is one principle in our Declaration of Independence which the American people have embraced with ardor, it is the pursuit of happiness. Sometimes, however, the chase takes on the feverish and desperate character of what is inelegantly described as a "rat race." Matthew Arnold used more polished words in speaking of the "sick hurry of modern life." There is danger, then, that we may escape from drudgery only to fall into idleness, disillusionment, and frustration. Americans are not people who are happy for long when they are doing nothing. There is no lasting happiness, on the other hand, in doing things that can only be recommended as a way to kill time. We need to remember that the word "leisure" derives from the Greek word meaning school. The prime use of leisure for adult human beings is through a happy discipline and training of the mind.

Here is where the humanities can play the role of liberator to the American spirit. They can train many Americans to practice the arts, sometimes professionally, often just for the personal pleasure they bring. They can teach many more millions of Americans to appreciate the arts, by which we mean experiencing vicariously what the artist experienced as he created or even something more than he experienced. Such genuine appreciaton enables one, as Professor Kermode says, to find out through a piece of literature or art "the unknown things about himself." In this way the arts will make men's lives genuinely happier.

Here, I am glad to say, the Congress of the United States has recently taken a relatively modest but nevertheless historic step. The House and Senate have passed a measure called "The National Arts and Humanities Act of 1965," and the President has signed it. The total expenditure proposed is only 21 million dollars the first year, a small item in our national budget. The purpose of the act is revolutionary, however. Some of the evidence cited at the Congressional hearings was exciting in the sense that the early statements of America's founding principles were exciting.

Let me read you a paragraph from the declaration made by a presidential Commission on the Humanities, a group of twenty outstanding humanists: "The humanities," they declared, "are the study of that which is most human. Throughout man's conscious past they have played an essential role in forming, preserving, and transforming the social, moral, and aesthetic values of every man in every age. One cannot speak of history or culture apart from the humanities. They not only record our lives; our lives are the very substance they are made of. Their subject is every man. We propose, therefore, a program for all our people, a program to meet a need no less serious than that for our national defense. We speak, in truth, for what is being defended—our beliefs, our ideals, our highest achievements."

Of course the Congress cannot pass a miracle as it passes a law and make America overnight a paradise of the humanities. The objective of this first Congressional act, however, is excellent. It is dedicated to this thesis: "That democracy demands wisdom and vision in its citizens and that it must therefore foster and support a form of education designed to make men masters of their technology and not its unthinking servants." President Johnson has acknowledged the limits of governmental action in the field of the arts. "No government," he concedes, "can call artistic excellence into existence. It must flow from the quality of the society and the good fortune of the nation. Nor should any government seek to restrain the freedom of the artist to pursue his calling in his own way. Freedom is an essential condition for the artist. . . . But government can seek to create conditions under which the arts can flourish; through recognition of achievements, through helping those who seek to enlarge creative understanding, through increasing the access of our people to the works of our artists, and through recognizing the arts as part of the pursuit of American greatness."

This leads me to my final point on America's need for a flowering of the humanities. We are confronted today with a curious irony of social history. On the one hand we have in America a society more broadly privileged, more liberated from monotonous toil, than any that this planet has known. On the other hand we have a society that seems haunted by unhappiness. Many young Americans, offered an amazing gamut of opportunities, flee from so baffling a choice to the oblivion of drugs or the refuge of the psychiatrist's couch. The old symbols of authority have been banished, as the statues of former rulers have been demolished in what were once colonial cities of Asia and Africa. Parents seldom exert the discipline over their children which was once the standard of family life. Many schools are so intent on seeing that young people enjoy themselves in the classroom that they overlook the enduring joy that comes from learning.

The churches of America show an all-time record of membership. Attendance, too, is high among well-dressed, well-fed and well-intentioned people. The tragedy is that so many Americans, and especially so many young Americans, find it impossible to accept the standards offered by organized religion. They cannot grasp the idea of a God "in whose service is perfect freedom." The ancient standards are still there, expressed with unparalleled nobility in the words of the Bible and in the rituals of all the varied churches. Other generations have found a source of strength in these precepts. Many young Americans have become completely deaf to them in the ceaseless din of modern life.

In the ancient human wisdom of religion there are answers to all the questions that plague young people everywhere. Here is the answer to their search for identity, for a pattern of meaning in life, for a security that extends beyond the possession of a "steady date" or a job or a ranch-house with a two-car garage. But many young people are embarrassed by the great truths of religion, and feel like hypocrites in a church to whose doctrines they cannot bring themselves to subscribe. Since they think of religion, to use Professor Frye's words, as "a dark preserve of mystery on which the sun of science has not risen," they reject its doctrines and hard obligations. It has been said that Americans are people who want to get to the promised land without passing through the wilderness. We are in a spiritual wilderness now, but we still have the ambition to achieve the high ground.

81

The trouble is that we have impatiently dismissed all the old guides and torn up the maps, because we wanted to be free of all restraining authority. We are free, all right—free to get lost and to wander in circles while the darkness begins to fall. A demand for freedom is running like a great tide around the world, and young Americans are caught in its powerful surge. In Indonesia they call it "merdekka," and crowds scream for it in the streets. In the old French colonies the cry has been for *liberté*. The words vary, but the fever and intoxication are everywhere the same. In some places the demand has been for political freedom, long denied and now passionately desired. Elsewhere the battle is for economic independence. Some Americans have been fighting, and some few of them dying, for the freedom to vote and to go to the same schools and hospitals with other Americans whose skin is a different color. That cause has aroused the idealism of many young, white Americans, to their eternal credit.

Some other young Americans, however, have concentrated on a drive for absolute individual freedom, freedom from all discipline and responsibility. Such unlimited liberty is not compatible with life in a civilized society. It is here that the humanities have something invaluable to offer to American life. The efforts of religion must and will of course continue unabated. But the humanities can to some extent share a job that needs all the help that can be mustered. The humanities, like religion, are not ashamed to erect standards of human behavior. They are not afraid to invoke the higher instincts of the human spirit. Plato sounded the call long ago, in the sunlight of Greece's glorious morning: "By education I mean the training in excellence from youth upwards which makes a man passionately desire to be a perfect citizen, and teaches him how to rule, and to obey, with justice."

Few people today would dare to speak in such exalted

terms—"training in excellence," "a perfect citizen," the ability either to rule or to obey "with justice." The aim of a humanistic education is not always proclaimed so unabashedly, but the goal has remained fundamentally the same through the ages. To Francis Bacon it was clear that "men should enter upon learning in order to give a true account of their gifts of reason, to the benefit and use of men." Even in the wasteland of the twentieth century, T. S. Eliot was able to make the same affirmation. "The natural end of man," he declared, "is virtue and well-being in the community."

The very word virtue has an archaic ring in the ears of young Americans. Yet in the sense that the great poets, philosophers and humanists have employed that word, I submit that it is the quality young Americans are blindly seeking at this moment. They blush at outward expressions of idealism, yet many of them eagerly embrace practical forms of idealism in modern life. I am thinking of the Peace Corps, of service in city slums and in lonely Appalachian valleys, or on the ragged battlefronts of the civil rights movement. The quality of idealism is still burning bright in the secret consciousness of millions of young Americans, though they are at pains to hide it behind a facade of "cool" behavior. They are longing to make a commitment to something far bigger than themselves, if they can only find it. They are in search of standards they have renounced without ever knowing their meaning. If they search too long without finding an object on which to focus their inner sense of dedication, they will turn into the cynical, bitter, frustrated adults of tomorrow.

I have urged a vigorous application of the humanities to American life for four reasons, but the last is the most vital. This is a work of liberation. The humanities have been committed to such a cause since the times of antiquity. They can yet, as Professor Beardsley says in his lecture, "enlarge and sensitize our ability to understand each other," without which enlargement and sensitization there can be no liberation, no freedom, of the human spirit. The old rallying cries are still vibrant, the banners still bright, the trumpets tuned to the call. It has always been the goal of the humanities to set men free. Now they must show the courage to help lead out of bondage an American generation that sold its inheritance for an illusion of freedom, but has found itself enslaved anew by its own fears and frustration.